Developing Proofreading Skill

Second Edition

Sue C. Camp, B.S., M.A.T., C.P.S.

Assistant Professor
Broyhill School of Management
Gardner-Webb College
Boiling Springs, North Carolina

Gregg Division
McGRAW-HILL BOOK COMPANY

New York Atlanta Dallas St. Louis San Francisco
Auckland Bogotá Guatemala Hamburg Lisbon
London Madrid Mexico Milan Montreal New Delhi
Panama Paris San Juan São Paulo Singapore
Sydney Tokyo Toronto

Sponsoring Editors: Marion B. Castellucci/Marie Orsini Rosen
Editing Supervisor: Vivian Koenig
Design and Art Supervisor: Meri Shardin
Production Supervisor: Albert H. Rihner

Text Designer: Suzanne Bennett & Associates
Cover Designer: Kurt Jennings
Technical Studio: Burmar Technical Corp.

Library of Congress Cataloging-in-Publication Data

Camp, Sue C., date
    Developing proofreading skill.

    Includes index.
    Summary: Outlines ways to detect typographical,
grammatical, and other common errors found in written
business communications.
    1. Proofreading.   2. English language—Business
English. (1. Proofreading.   2. Commercial correspondence.
3. English language—Business English)   I. Title.
Z254.C35   1987   808   86-18085
ISBN 0-07-009727-5

        3 4 5 6 7 8 9 0   WEBWEB   8 9 3 2 1 0 9 8

ISBN 0-07-009727-5

Contents

Chapter 12
Correcting Inconsistencies   128

Preface

"You never get a second chance to make a first impression" is an adage often quoted in business circles. Although this adage usually relates to a personal, first-time meeting—such as a job interview—it has great relevance to written business communications.

The business letter, for example, may be the first meeting your company has with a potential customer. Through that letter, your company has the opportunity to create a positive first impression and thereby encourage the potential customer to become a new customer and subsequently a satisfied customer.

Proofreading skill will help your business letters and other written communications not only to create that good first impression but also to maintain it throughout the business relationship.

Proofreading skill must be developed. It is an important skill for *all* members of the business writing team: transcribers, dictators, word processing operators, stenographers, typists, and writers themselves. Efficient proofreaders know the importance of finding and correcting errors. They also know *how* to find errors and *where* errors are frequently made but overlooked.

Developing Proofreading Skill, Second Edition, will provide you with the instruction and practice needed to improve your skill. In this program, the exercises will gradually increase in difficulty as your skill improves. The exercises will introduce you to realistic business communications—such as letters, memorandums, messages, expense reports, agendas, and résumés—that you will encounter on the job. You will learn the standard way of marking needed changes. You will also learn ways to mark changes for printing options (like boldface print) that have become available on electronic equipment.

Because of our technological age, much of what is keyboarded today involves numbers and specialized terms. This second edition of *Developing Proofreading Skill* offers a chapter on proofreading statistical and technical documents.

Also new with this edition is software. Instructions for using the software are at the back of this book. There and throughout the text, you will find instructions and much practice material on proofreading printed or typed documents. The software offers the challenge of proofreading these documents on the word processing screen as well.

Whether you plan to start work soon or are already on the job, you will certainly need to develop your proofreading skill. With instruction and practice, you can learn to produce written messages more quickly and accurately. Let's get started!

Acknowledgments

The following outstanding educators reviewed *Developing Proofreading Skill,* Second Edition. Their participation is evidence of their expertise and commitment to business education.

Jean M. Chappell, North Knox Vocational Center, Knoxville, Tennessee

Gary Gebhart, Great Oaks Joint Vocational School District, Cincinnati, Ohio

Homer M. Hayes, San Antonio College, San Antonio, Texas

Genevieve L. Stelling, Manor College, Jenkintown, Pennsylvania

Sue C. Camp

Typographical Errors

Proofreading Names, Addresses, and Telephone Numbers

NAMES

Names, addresses, and telephone numbers appear frequently in the routine performance of daily office work. Business people expect to have their names spelled correctly. Proofread the following pairs of names to teach yourself to be alert to potential errors in names. As you proofread this list or any other list of names, be sure to follow these pointers:

▼▼ Proofreading Pointers

▼ Check the spelling of each part of a person's name (first, middle, last), and check initials.

▼ Verify possible alternate spellings of names (for example, Frances or Francis? Lynn or Lynne?).

▼ When using courtesy titles, make sure the appropriate one is used: Mr., Ms., Miss, Mrs., or Dr.

● **1-1**   Are the names in Columns A and B identical? If they are, write *yes* in the space provided. If they are not, write *no* in the space. (10 points each correct answer)

A	B	Yes/No?
1. Gerald R. Carroll	Gerald R. Caroll	1. _____
2. Janice Marie Stevenson	Janice Marie Stevenson	2. _____
3. Dr. Alicia Goldberg	Dr. Alicia Goldberg	3. _____
4. Mr. H. Steven Gilbert	Mr. H. Stephen Gilbert	4. _____
5. Mrs. Andrew J. Billingsly	Mrs. Andrew J. Billingsly	5. _____

A	B	Yes/No?
6. Dexter L. Ortega	Dexter K. Ortega	6. _____
7. Ms. Nichole Ashley-Kline	Ms. Nichole Ashley-Kline	7. _____
8. Dr. Francisco Delgado	Dr. Francesca Delgado	8. _____
9. Miss Catherine Warner	Mrs. Catherine Warner	9. _____
10. Thomas Leonard Hilliard	Thomas Leonard Hilliard	10. _____

STATE ABBREVIATIONS

The U.S. Postal Service has established two-letter abbreviations for states, territories, and possessions of the United States. Even though these abbreviations were created for addressing envelopes, most business writers also use these abbreviations in the inside addresses of letters. (When the name of a state appears in the text of a letter, it is usually not abbreviated.)

Note the following example. When using the two-letter state abbreviations, type them in capital letters, with no periods after or space between the letters.

Mrs. Miriam Crosby
Crosby and Company
Post Office Box 3254
Kansas City, KS 66103

For a quick reference, a list of these abbreviations is provided on the inside back cover of this book.

● **1-2** Using the list on the inside back cover, list the two-letter abbreviation for each of the following states. Remember to use capital letters. (5 points each correct answer)

1. California	1. _____	11. Connecticut	11. _____
2. Maine	2. _____	12. Alaska	12. _____
3. Florida	3. _____	13. Ohio	13. _____
4. Guam	4. _____	14. North Dakota	14. _____
5. Rhode Island	5. _____	15. Indiana	15. _____
6. Utah	6. _____	16. Minnesota	16. _____
7. Texas	7. _____	17. Kentucky	17. _____
8. Arizona	8. _____	18. Mississippi	18. _____
9. Louisiana	9. _____	19. Nevada	19. _____
10. Michigan	10. _____	20. Delaware	20. _____

● **1-3** Is the abbreviation listed in Column B the correct two-letter abbreviation for the state or territory listed in Column A? If so, write *yes* in the space provided. If not, write *no* in the space, and write the correct abbreviation beside your answer. Refer to the list on the inside back cover to check abbreviations. (5 points each correct item)

A	B	Yes/No?	Correct Abbreviation
Example:			
0. Hawaii	HA	0. No	HI
1. Wyoming	WO	1. _____	_____

	A	B	Yes/No?	Correct Abbreviation
2.	Alabama	AL	2. _____	_____
3.	North Carolina	NC	3. _____	_____
4.	Wisconsin	WS	4. _____	_____
5.	Oklahoma	OK	5. _____	_____
6.	Illinois	ILL	6. _____	_____
7.	Maryland	MD	7. _____	_____
8.	Missouri	MO	8. _____	_____
9.	Vermont	VT	9. _____	_____
10.	Tennessee	TN	10. _____	_____
11.	Colorado	CL	11. _____	_____
12.	West Virginia	WV	12. _____	_____
13.	Nebraska	NA	13. _____	_____
14.	Kansas	KA	14. _____	_____
15.	New Jersey	NJ	15. _____	_____
16.	Oregon	OR	16. _____	_____
17.	Iowa	IA	17. _____	_____
18.	Virgin Islands	VI	18. _____	_____
19.	District of Columbia	DC	19. _____	_____
20.	Virginia	VR	20. _____	_____

ZIP CODES

ZIP Codes have been used for years to help get mail to the right place more quickly. Now, the U.S. Postal Service has added four digits to create the ZIP+4 Code: 02914-6212. These last four digits can be used to designate an office in a large building, an industrial park complex, or a specific household in a community.

The Postal Service particularly encourages businesses to use the additional four digits and suggests that reprints of company stationery include the ZIP+4 Code. Proofreading ZIP Codes and ZIP+4 Codes has become increasingly important because the post office uses optical character reading equipment to scan these numbers, which permits automatic sorting of mail.

Now that you know that ZIP Codes are a necessary part of an address, be alert to incorrect ZIP Codes in the proofreading exercises in the rest of this book.

● **1-4** Compare the ZIP Codes and ZIP+4 Codes in Column A with the ones in Column B. If they are identical, write *yes* in the space provided. If not, write *no* in the space, and write the Column A number beside your answer. Be sure to proofread the numbers you write in the correct number column. (10 points each item)

	A	B	Yes/No?	Correct Number
Example:				
0.	28017	28018	0. No	28017
1.	70127	70227	1. _____	_____

A	B	Yes/No?	Correct Number
2. 02178	02178	2. _____	_____
3. 48507	48507	3. _____	_____
4. 63105	63100	4. _____	_____
5. 14626	15626	5. _____	_____
6. 15904-6612	15004-6612	6. _____	_____
7. 77017-1437	77017-1438	7. _____	_____
8. 84119-1521	84110-1511	8. _____	_____
9. 23605-8513	23605-8513	9. _____	_____
10. 53715-7116	53715-7661	10. _____	_____

● **1-5** Are the items in Column B identical to the ones in Column A? Write the correct answer, *yes* or *no*, in the space provided. (10 points each correct answer)

A	B	Yes/No?
1. Athens, GA 30601	Athens, GA 30601	1. _____
2. Lansing, MI 48917	Lensing, MI 48917	2. _____
3. Baltimore, MD 21204-2489	Baltimore, MD 21204-2489	3. _____
4. Wilson, WY 83104	Wilson, WY 83104	4. _____
5. Durham, NC 27704	Durham, NC 27704	5. _____
6. Lubbock, TX 79401-8672	Lubbock, TX 79401-8672	6. _____
7. Racine, WI 53405	Racine, WI 53405	7. _____
8. Passaic, NJ 07057	Passaic, NY 07057	8. _____
9. Newport News, VA 23605	Newport News, VA 23605	9. _____
10. Everett, WA 98203-3498	Everett, WA 98203-3498	10. _____

● **1-6** Compare the handwritten and typewritten items. If they are the same, write *yes* in the space provided. If they are different, write *no* in the space provided. (10 points each correct answer)

A	B	Yes/No?
1. *Dr. Paul C. Goldstein*	Mr. Paul C. Goldstein	1. _____
2. *Alice C. O'Malley*	Alice C. O'Nalley	2. _____
3. *Mrs. Anne Parsons*	Mrs. Anne Parsons	3. _____
4. *Thomas P. Connor*	Thomas P. Conor	4. _____
5. *Belle Marie Bankoff*	Belle Marie Bankoff	5. _____
6. *E. Providence, RI 02914*	East Providence, RI 02914	6. _____
7. *Decatur, GA 30032*	Decatur, GA 30032	7. _____
8. *Eugene, OR 97401-4425*	Eugene, OP 97401-4425	8. _____
9. *Bellevue, WA 98009*	Belleuue, WA 98009	9. _____
10. *Harrisburg, PA 1603-2214*	Harrisburg, PA 1693-2214	10. _____

COMPLETE ADDRESSES

An address should have this information:

Example

Name of addressee and title	Mrs. Susan P. Brennan, President
Company name (if appropriate)	Brennan Manufacturing Company
Street address (or post office box number)	2034 Cranston Drive
City, state abbreviation, ZIP Code	Shelby, NC 28150

The addressee's title may be typed on the same line as his or her name, as in the example, or it may be typed on a separate line.

After the city name, type a comma, space once, type the two-letter state abbreviation in capital letters, space once, and type the ZIP Code or the ZIP + 4 Code.

● **1-7** Are the addresses in Column B identical to the addresses in Column A? Write the correct response, *yes* or *no*, in the space provided. (10 points each correct answer)

A	B	Yes/No?
1. Mr. and Mrs. Adam Riggs 1031 Ravenswood Drive Evansville, IN 47714	Mr. and Mrs. Adam Riggs 1031 Ravenswood Drive Evanville, IN 47714	1. _____
2. Mrs. Ellen B. Cohen Post Office Box 1897 Annapolis, MD 21404	Mrs. Ellen D. Cohen Post Office Box 1897 Annapolis, MD 21404	2. _____
3. Ms. Benita Gonzales 1905 East 43rd Street Akron, OH 44305	Ms. Benita Gonzales 1905 East 434d Street Akron, OH 44305	3. _____
4. Mr. Stan Brewster 1530 Robin Drive Oklahoma City, OK 73101	Mr. Stan Brewster 1530 Robin Drive Oklahoma City, OK 73101	4. _____
5. Mrs. June McDonald 1261 Parkview Drive Grand Rapids, MI 49506–4461	Ms. June McDonald 1261 Parkview Drive Grand Rapids, MI 49506–4461	5. _____
6. Ms. Nancy Dubois, President Quality Publishing Company Post Office Box 10030 Cincinnati, OH 45210	Ms. Nancy Dubois, President Quality Publishing Company Post Office Box 10030 Cincinnati, OH 45210	6. _____
7. Mr. and Mrs. Moses Steinberg Condominium Village 1321 Essex Street Manchester, NH 03102	Mr. and Mrs. Moses Steinberg Condominium Village 1321 Essex Street Manchester, NH 03102	7. _____
8. Mr. Fred Roberts 1405 Elizabeth Road Kansas City, KS 67218	Mr. Fred Roberts 1405 Elizabeth Road Kansas City, KS 67218	8. _____
9. Dr. Vanessa O'Reilly Metro Professional Building 1530 Robinwood Drive Oklahoma City, OK 73101–4530	Dr. Vanessa O'Reilly Metro Professional Building 1530 Robinwood Drive Oklahoma City, OH 73101–4530	9. _____

A	B	Yes/No?
10. Mrs. Leslie Girard 101 Abington Avenue Philadelphia, PA 19118	Mrs. Leslie Girard 101 Abington Avenue Philadelphia, PA 19188	10. _____

TELEPHONE NUMBERS

An error in recording or transcribing a telephone number can be costly. A search for the correct number can be both time-consuming and fruitless. Keeping in mind the importance of accurately recording, reporting, and proofreading numbers, complete the exercise below. These pointers will help you proofread telephone numbers:

▼▼ Proofreading Pointers

▼ Read each telephone number in parts; for example, read the number (704) 555-9322 in three parts: "seven-zero-four, five-five-five, nine-three-two-two."

▼ When proofreading columns of numbers, check that all parts—such as parentheses, hyphens, spaces—are aligned.

▼ Check that each number has the appropriate number of digits. Area codes, for example, have three digits. The rest of the telephone number should have seven digits, three before and four after the hyphen.

● **1-8** Compare the telephone numbers in Columns A and B. If they are identical, write *yes* in the space provided. If they are different, write *no* in the space. (10 points each correct answer)

A	B	Yes/No?
1. (206) 992-4581	(206) 992-4581	1. _____
2. (503) 472-7790	(503) 472-790	2. _____
3. (405) 782-6687	(405) 82-6687	3. _____
4. (215) 923-8811	(215) 923-8811	4. _____
5. (701) 314-3398	(701) 314-3389	5. _____
6. (303) 728-7878	(303) 728-7878	6. _____
7. (912) 997-9923	(921) 997-9923	7. _____
8. (602) 874-5597	(602) 874-5597	8. _____
9. (319) 785-6498	(39) 785-6498	9. _____
10. (316) 643-6655	(316) 643-6655	10. _____

Proofreading for Omissions and Repetitions

As business communications are transcribed or copied, letters, words, or even entire lines may be omitted or repeated. Such errors are common, even with automated equipment. Moreover, they may go unnoticed; for example, when a sentence can make sense without a missing word. As you can see, then, you must be careful to proofread for copy that may be omitted.

When you are proofreading, however, you must read for more than sense; you must read for accuracy. The following sentences make sense, but one of each pair definitely has an error.

I do not want to attend the meeting in Australia.
I do want to attend the meeting in Australia.

I have enclosed my check for $85.
I have enclosed my check for $885.

Quite a difference! Be careful to look for omitted and repeated letters, numbers, words, and lines.

The proofreaders' mark used to indicate that copy has been omitted is the caret (∧).

Send the contract to Mrs. Har∧mon.   *t*
You should ∧work late every night.   *not*
Mail ∧copies to all corporate officers.   *two*

Mark repetition errors as follows:

The United States has 50ᴓ states.

Can we give the awards next weeᴓk?

Most of the ~~the~~ delay was caused by bad weather.

Now, let's test your ability to find omissions and repetitions. The first paragraph is correct. Proofread the second paragraph to make it correct too. Use the caret to indicate any missing letters or words. Strike through repetitions as shown above.

```
     Please send me 15 more
copies of Planning for Expansion
by Lester Kiley. We are using
this excellent book in our
management training program.
```

```
     Please send me 155 more
of Plannning for Expansion by
by Lester Kiley. We are using
this book in our managment
training program.
```

Did you notice that there were two words omitted, *copies* (line 2) and *excellent* (line 4)? Did you also notice that underscores were omitted in the book title (line 2)? Did you see that *managment* (line 4) should be *management*? Notice, too, that the paragraph makes sense without the words *copies* and *excellent*.

Did you notice these repetitions: *155* for *15* (line 1); *Plannning* for *Planning* (line 2); and *by* repeated (line 3)?

▼▼ Proofreading Pointers

▼ Look for omission and repetition errors especially at the ends and beginnings of lines and pages.

▼ Read for accuracy and meaning.

Omissions and repetitions occur frequently in copy produced on word processing equipment. Word processing programs allow corrections on the screen such as moving text (words, sentences, and even paragraphs). The omission error occurs when the text is deleted from its first location and not reinserted into the copy.

Example:

Most of our employees prefer four days instead of five days per week to work.

Suppose you wanted to move *to work* so that it appears between *prefer* and *four*. If the words *to work* were deleted from their first location and not inserted in their correct location, the sentence would be as follows:

Most of our employees prefer four days instead of five days per week.

Repetitions can occur on automated equipment when the text is correctly inserted in its new location but not deleted from its original location.

Most of our employees prefer to work four days instead of five days per week to work.

You are now familiar with some of the ways that omissions and repetitions occur in day-to-day business communications. Be alert to these throughout the rest of the book.

Now, let's test your ability to find repetitions and omissions in the next exercise.

● **1-9** The paragraphs in Column A are correct. Proofread the paragraphs in Column B to find any omissions or repetitions. Mark your corrections as shown in this chapter. Write *yes* in the space provided if the paragraph in Column B is correct. Write *no* if it is not correct. (20 points each paragraph)

A	B	Yes/No?
1. Please consider this letter an application for employment with your firm. In just two weeks I will receive my bachelor of science degree in business adminis-tration from State College, and I am most eager to put my education to work.	Please consider this letter an application for employment with with your firm. In just two weeks I will receive my bachelor of science degree from State College, and I am most eager to put my eduction am most eager to put my education to work.	1._____
2. Your packaging idea for our computer software certainly merits consideration by our marketing staff. We value consumer comments and many times are able to use them.	Your packaging idea for our computer software certainly merits consideration by our marketinging staff. We value consumer comments and many times are able to to use them.	2._____
3. Last week our company ordered 500 nylon jackets with our company emblem on them. The jackets were delivered today, but our competitor's emblem was printed on each one. Need-less to say, these jackets are of no use to us, and we would appreciate your let-	Last week our company ordered 50 nylon jackets with our company emblem on them. The jackets were delivered today, but our competitor's emblem was printed on each one. Need-Needless to say, these jackets are of no use to us, and we and we would appreciate your leting us know when to expect jackets and what to do with the ones shipped to us in errorr.	

| A | B | Yes/No? |

ting us know when to expect
our jackets and what to do
with the ones shipped to us
in error.

3._____

4.   Your Invoice 4314, dated
October 5, 1986, was received
in our Atlanta office yesterday.
Please notice that the amount
we owe your company, $31.12,
is incorrectly typed as $311.20.
Our check for $31.12 is enclosed
to cover our account in full.

    Your Invoice 4314 date
October 5, 1986, was received in
in our Atlanta office yesterday.
Please notice that the amount
we owe our company, $31.12,
is incorrectly typed as $311.20.
Our check is enclosed to cover
our account in full.

4._____

5.   Our current absentee
rate is quite high. Since
absenteeism increases our
costs and decreases our
quality, please prepare a
report including your suggestions for better controlling
absenteeism. We will discuss
your report at our regular
meeting.

    Our current absentee rate is
quite high. Since absenteeism increases our costs and decreases
our quality, please prepare a
report including your suggestions
for better controlling absenteeism.
We will discuss your report at our
regular meeting.

5._____

Proofreading Numbers

Reading, reporting, and keyboarding numbers accurately is essential in efficient business communications. Numbers are used frequently in writing ages, dates, decimal fractions, dollar amounts, times of day, and weights and measures. Regardless of how the figures are used, train your eyes and mind to be accurate.

Why are numbers important? Consider the consequences of the following number errors:

1. On Mrs. Herndon's medical chart, you list her weight as 191 instead of 119.

2. On your employer's travel itinerary, you indicate the plane departure time as 10:50. You should have listed it as 10:05. Your employer would probably arrive at the boarding gate just in time to see the plane take off.

3. At the peak of the winter tourist season, you make hotel reservations at a convention center for January 22–29 instead of January 21–29. Perhaps your employer will have time to "cool off" while spending the first night of the business trip on the sofa in the center lobby.

Here are some proofreading pointers that will help you find errors in numbers:

▼▼ Proofreading Pointers

▼ After reading a communication for content and mechanics (grammar, spell-ing, and punctuation), check all numbers in a separate step.

▼ Make sure that numbers make sense. For example, an article stating that someone retired at age 16 probably reported the age incorrectly.

▼ Check that columns of numbers align (hyphens under hyphens, decimals under decimals, etc.).

▼ When proofreading several columns of numbers, read down each column, not across from left to right. For example, proofread columns of phone numbers by reading the area codes down each column, then the next three numbers (called the "exchange"), and then the last four numbers.

▼ Make sure that numbers have the appropriate number of digits. Social security numbers have nine digits separated by hyphens in this pattern: 000-00-0000. Phone numbers have ten digits in this pattern (000) 000-0000.

▼ To double-check retyped columns of numbers, quickly add the numbers in the first draft. Then add the numbers in the final copy. The totals should be the same. This method works well when proofreading final copies keyboarded from handwritten originals.

To increase your alertness to potential errors in numbers, complete this exercise:

● **1-10** In the following list, two of the three items are identical and one is different. Identify the different item by writing the column heading, *A*, *B*, or *C*, in the space provided. (5 points each correct answer)

	A	B	C	
1.	Page 489	Page 489	Page 589	1. _____
2.	11:50 a.m.	11:05 a.m.	11:50 a.m.	2. _____
3.	$2,457.84	$2,457.85	$2,457.84	3. _____
4.	12-8-87	11-8-87	11-8-87	4. _____
5.	January 22, 1986	January 22, 1987	January 22, 1986	5. _____
6.	3 years 5 months 9 days old	3 years 5 months 9 days old	3 years 5 months 19 days old	6. _____
7.	Aged 18	Aged 18	Aged 28	7. _____
8.	10-18-88	10-28-88	10-28-88	8. _____
9.	a room 14 by 18 feet	a room 14 by 19 feet	a room 14 by 19 feet	9. _____
10.	$145.14	$144.14	$144.14	10. _____
11.	72,4312.63428	72,4312.63429	72,4312.63429	11. _____
12.	April 29, 1989	April 29, 1989	April 29, 1988	12. _____
13.	1985–1990	1985–1990	1985–1980	13. _____
14.	0.70 gram	0.07 gram	0.07 gram	14. _____
15.	$33,433.65	$33,433.67	$33,433.65	15. _____
16.	December 9, 1968	December 9, 1968	December 9, 1969	16. _____
17.	10 7/16	10 8/16	10 7/16	17. _____
18.	Pages 223–256	Pages 223–257	Pages 223–256	18. _____
19.	17.967 percent	17.867 percent	17.867 percent	19. _____
20.	$1,986.78	$1,987.78	$1,986.78	20. _____

Proofreading Review

Try your proofreading skill as you do the following exercises. Exercise 1-A provides additional practice for material included in Chapter 1. Exercise 1-B is a practical application that you might see in an actual business situation.

● **1-A** Are the items in Columns A and B identical? If they are, write *yes* in the space provided. If they are not, write *no*. (2 points each correct answer)

	A	B	Yes/No?
Names			
1.	Mr. Christopher Rosenberg	Mr. Christopher Rosenberg	1. _____
2.	J. William Walsh	J. William Walsh	2. _____
3.	Miss Grayson B. Harrison	Miss Grayson B. Harrison	3. _____
4.	Mrs. Roberto Alverez Sanchos	Mr. Roberto Alverez Sanchos	4. _____
5.	Dr. Sarah Lynn Hawks	Dr. Sarah Lynn Hawks	5. _____
6.	Mr. John W. Logan	Mr. John W. Logan	6. _____
7.	R. Jonathan Tolbert	R. Jonathan Tolbert	7. _____
8.	Ms. Edith Elizabeth Renslo	Ms. Edith Elisabeth Renslo	8. _____
9.	Miss Lisa Ann Foxx	Miss Lisa Ann Foxx	9. _____
10.	Allison R. Ellingberg	Allison B. Ellingberg	10. _____
ZIP Codes			
11.	39530	39530	11. _____
12.	87105	87105	12. _____
13.	76310–4489	76310–4489	13. _____
14.	48604–2398	48604–1298	14. _____
15.	28206	28206	15. _____
16.	33612	33622	16. _____
17.	29602	29601	17. _____
18.	06031	06013	18. _____
19.	15205–2156	15205–2156	19. _____
20.	95126–3167	95126–3168	20. _____

Addresses

21. Mr. Peter John Bannister
Accounts Payable Department
Professional Software, Inc.
1995 Amherst Drive
Manchester, NH 03104

Mr. Peter Jon Bannister
Accounts Payable Department
Professional Software, Inc.
1995 Amherst Drive
Manchester, NH 03104

21. _____

Addresses

22. Mrs. Susan Livingstone
    Office Temporaries
    Post Office Box 2997
    Biloxi, MS 39531

    Mrs. Susan Livingston
    Office Temporaries
    Post Office Box 2997
    Biloxi, MS 29531   22. _____

23. Ms. Francine Mauney
    Attorney-at-Law
    892 Hanover Drive
    Waterbury, CT 0614-0892

    Ms. Francine Mauney
    Attorney-at Law
    8922 Hanover Drive
    Waterbury, CT 0614-0892   23. _____

24. Dr. G. Morgan Prescott
    Medical Associates, PA
    7728 Ocean Highway
    Honolulu, HI 96819

    Mr. G. Morgan Prescott
    Medical Associates, PA
    7728 Ocean Highway
    Honolulu, HI 96819   24. _____

25. Mr. Sam Batavia
    Batavia and Associates
    2285 Baxter Avenue
    Gary, IN 46402

    Mr. Sam Batavia
    Batavia and Associates
    2285 Baxter Avenue
    Gary, IN 46402   25. _____

26. Mr. David M. Hilton
    Vice President
    City National Bank
    Post Office Box 1106
    Duluth, MN 55801

    Mr. David N. Hilton
    Vice President
    City National Bank
    Post Office Box 1106
    Duluth, MN 55801   26. _____

27. Mr. Abraham Fitzhugh
    Chairman of the Board
    Real Estate Investments, Inc.
    3299 Badger Road
    Arlington Heights, IL 60005

    Mr. Abraham Fitzhugh
    Chairman of the Board
    Real Estate Investments, Inc.
    3299 Badger Road
    Arlington Heights, IL 60005 27. _____

28. Mrs. Linda Manning-Jones
    City News and Observer
    1829 Byron Street
    New York, NY 14422-1829

    Mrs. Linda Manning-Jones
    City News and Observer
    1829 Byron Street
    New York, NY 14422-1839   28. _____

29. Miss Julia Duquette
    8725 Independence Boulevard
    Charlotte, NC 28202

    Miss Julia Duquette
    8725 Independence Boulevard
    Charlotte, NC 28202   29. _____

30. Mr. Benton R. O'Reilly
    Floral Designers, Inc.
    Post Office Box 6649
    Kansas City, KS 66104

    Mr. Benton R. O'Reilly
    Floral Designers, Inc.
    Post Office Box 6649
    Kansas City, KN 66104   30. _____

Telephone Numbers

31. (208) 482-5878   (208) 482-5878   31. _____
32. (801) 842-8722   (801) 842-8822   32. _____
33. (304) 782-9168   (304) 782-0168   33. _____
34. (919) 337-7492   (919) 377-7492   34. _____
35. (203) 538-6523   (203) 538-6523   35. _____
36. (208) 785-7238   (208) 785-7238   36. _____
37. (605) 398-7727   (605) 398-7728   37. _____
38. (402) 924-6733   (402) 924-6733   38. _____

Telephone Numbers (*continued*)

39. (904) 582–9166	(944) 582–9166	39. _____
40. (413) 882–4488	(413) 882–4588	40. _____

Numbers

41. 11:55 p.m.	11:55 p.m.	41. _____
42. $235,468.89	$245,468.89	42. _____
43. Hotel Room 2913	Hotel Room 2313	43. _____
44. 1986–1991	1986–1992	44. _____
45. Pages 165–219	Pages 165–219	45. _____
46. 2.18 grams	2.18 grams	46. _____
47. 10–30–88	10–30–88	47. _____
48. 2/10, n/30	2/10, n/30	48. _____
49. March 28, 1987	March 29, 1987	49. _____
50. 15.5 ounces	15.5 ounces	50. _____

● **1-B** As credit manager, you asked your word processing operator to keyboard and print lists of overdue accounts. List 1, below, includes accounts from January 1 to January 15. List 2, on the next page, includes accounts from January 16 to January 31. You asked that the list be arranged in chronological order with the account longest overdue at the top and the account least overdue at the bottom. The new lists would include the name and address of each customer, the amount past due, and the date the amount was due.

Use the caret (∧) to correct omissions, and strike through repetitions (book~~y~~ and the ~~the~~). Make a small check (✓) beside the date of each entry that is completely correct. (10 points each correct check mark and correction)

OLD LIST 1

Ms. Barbara Gresham
Post Office Box 83384
Lincoln, NE 68501

$11,382.56
January 15 _____

Mr. Russell Hollis
3614 Montview Street
Lowell, MA 01851–1614

$13,295.32
January 12 _____

Mr. Phillip Jayhawk
Jayhawk's Landscaping Company
1422 Auburn Avenue
Wichita, KS 67219

$12,856.21
January 10 _____

Mrs. Sybil Lyndhurst
551 Johnston Avenue
Rockford, IL 61103–2551

$851.14
January 5 _____

NEW LIST 1 KEYBOARDED BY WORD PROCESSING OPERATOR

Mrs. Sybil Lyndhurst
551 Johnston Avenue
Rockford, IL 61103–25511

$852.14
January 5 _____

Mr. Phillip Jayhawk
Jayhawk's Landscaping Company
1422 Auburn Avenue
Wichita, KS 67219

$12,856.21
January 10 _____

Mr. Russell Hollis
3614 Montview Street
Lowell, MA 01851–1614

$13,295.32
Jannuary 12 _____

Ms. Barbara Gresham
Post Office 83384
Lincoln, NE 68501

$11,382.56
January 15 _____

(*continued*)

(continued)

OLD LIST 2

Dr. Mildred McCurdy
Metroview Medical Center
Office 1004
Olympia, WA 98503-5729

$12,819.65
January 29 _____

Mr. William T. Schaeffer
18225 Teakwood Boulevard
Amarillo, TX 79107

$437.99
January 25 _____

Mr. L. C. Shaughnessey
1425 Monarch Road
Cleveland, OH 44121

$898.44
January 22 _____

Mr. Wendel H. Weikert
Post Office Box 5422
Lancaster, PA 17601

$12,573.67
January 27 _____

Miss Hayden Wexler
9148 Wilcox Court
Arlington, VA 22310

$15,739.09
January 30 _____

**NEW LIST 2 KEYBOARDED BY
WORD PROCESSING OPERATOR**

Mr. L. C. Shaughnesey
1425 Monarch Road
Cleveland, OH 44121

$898.44
January 22 _____

Mr. William T. Schaeffer
18225 Teakwood Boulevard
Amarillo, TX 79107

$437.99
January 25 _____

Mr. Wendel H. Weikert
Post Office Box Box 5422
Lancaster, PA 17601

$12,573.67
January 27 _____

Mr. William T. Schaeffer
18225 Teakwood Boulevard
Amarillo, TX 79107

$437.99
January 25 _____

Dr. Mildred McCurdy
Metroview Medical Center
Office 1004
Olympia, WA 98503

$12,819.65
January 29 _____

Miss Hayden Wexler
9148 Wilcox Court
Arlington, VA 22310

$15,739.09
January 30 _____

More Typographical Errors

Proofreading for Transpositions

Many of the errors found in business writing are typographical or keyboarding errors. In other words, the person keyboarding (often called *keying*) a document simply strikes the wrong key. Some of these errors are very obvious; others escape detection frequently.

Whether proofreading your own work or the work of others, you will avoid unnecessary embarrassment by finding and correcting errors rather than having them pointed out by your employer or a customer. Most business executives encourage their employees to find and correct errors. It is the undetected, uncorrected errors that executives find unacceptable.

Transpositions, sometimes called *turnarounds,* are common. These are rearrangements of the correct order of letters, words, or numbers. Two common examples of letter transpositions are *hte* for *the* and *form* for *from.* The *hte* is easy to detect, but the word *form* for *from* is missed by both proofreaders and "spelling checker" software because although *form* is the wrong word, it is a correctly spelled word. "Spelling checker" software (a program used on automated equipment and designed to detect spelling errors) will not find the error because its dictionary recognizes the word as correctly spelled.

Words, too, may be transposed. For example, *and on so* is often substituted for *and so on.* Number transpositions are also common. The number (212) 867-4497 may be keyed when the correct number is (212) 867-4479.

Transpositions should be marked as indicated below:

hte   form   and on so   (212) 867-4497

This proofreaders' mark indicates that the two items should change places.

In Chapter 1, three proofreaders' marks were introduced. The caret (∧) was used to insert a word or a letter; the delete mark (✗) was used to omit an unnecessary letter (office); and a horizontal line was used to strike through unnecessary words (that ~~that~~). These proofreaders' marks, along with others used in this book, are shown on the inside back cover.

Exercises 2-1 and 2-2 will give you practice in finding transpositions.

▼▼ Proofreading Pointers

▼ Proofreading backward (from left to right) makes typographical errors more obvious.

▼ Be alert to a common keyboarding error—transpositions of letters, numbers, and words.

● **2-1**   Are the names and Social Security numbers in Columns A and B identical? If they are, answer *yes* in the space provided. If they are different, write *no* in the space. (10 points each correct item)

A	B	Yes/No?
1. Nelson R. Cranston 584-66-4482	Nelson R. Cranston 584-66-4428	1. _____
2. Linda Dillon Barcelona 239-67-1947	Linda Dillon Barcelona 239-67-1947	2. _____
3. R. Lester Fraley 562-89-5839	R. Lester Fraley 562-98-5839	3. _____
4. Jennifer Parks-Baker 349-86-2367	Jennifre Parks-Baker 349-86-2367	4. _____
5. Susan Pratt Freidberg 219-48-5398	Susan Pratt Friedberg 219-483-5398	5. _____
6. Dennis F. Williamson 287-32-3927	Dennis F. Williamson 287-32-3927	6. _____
7. Ronald Bradley Davis 439-33-7409	Ronald Bradley Davis 439-33-7402	7. _____
8. Alberto F. Rodriquez 367-88-3399	Ablerto F. Rodriquez 367-88-3399	8. _____
9. Louis P. Margoli 589-35-8042	Louis P. Margoli 589-35-8402	9. _____
10. Mitchelle Vance Dupree 624-63-0578	Michelle Vance Dupree 624-63-0578	10. _____

● **2-2**   Use the correct proofreaders' mark (ꞔ⃝ and (on so)) to mark transpositions in the following pairs. Assume that the first item in each group is correct and that the second item has the transposition. (10 points each correct item)

1. 254-87-3491
   254–87–3419

2. (804) 619-3408
   (804) 619–4308

3. Decatur, GA 30032
   Decatur, GA 30023

4. Fort Pierce, FL 33450
   Fort Peirce, FL 33450

5. Houston, TX 77001-5320
   Houston, TX 77001—3520

6. Athens, GA 30601-4215
   Ahtens, GA 30601—4215

7. All files are now stored on computer disk.
   All flies are now stored on computer disk.

8. Can we use their advertising campaign to sell our products?
   Can we use their advertising campiagn to sell
   our products?

9. Many of the latest technological advancements have made work easier.
   Many the of latest technological advancements
   have made work easier.

10. Your productivity rate has exceeded all of our expectations.
    Your productivity rate has exceeded all our of
    expectations.

Proofreading for Correct Spacing

Standard spacing is important in making sure that communications are correct. Review the following summary of spacing with punctuation marks, and then complete the exercises that follow.

1. There is no space before:
   a. An apostrophe within a word
   b. A comma
   c. A semicolon
   d. A colon
   e. A closing quotation mark
   f. A closing bracket
   g. A closing parenthesis
2. There is no space after:
   a. A period when followed by another punctuation mark
   b. A question mark when followed by another punctuation mark
   c. An exclamation point when followed by another punctuation mark
   d. An opening bracket or parenthesis
   e. An opening quotation mark
   f. A closing bracket or parenthesis when followed by another punctuation mark
   g. An asterisk in a footnote
   h. An apostrophe within a word
3. There are no spaces before or after:
   a. An apostrophe within a word
   b. A decimal point within a number
   c. Two hyphens representing a dash within a sentence
   d. A colon expressing time or ratio
   e. A diagonal
   f. A comma within a number
4. There is no space between:
   a. A punctuation mark and closing quotation marks
   b. Single and double quotation marks
   c. Two hyphens used as a dash

5. There is one space before:
   a. An opening bracket within a sentence
   b. An opening parenthesis within a sentence
   c. An opening quotation mark within a sentence
6. There are two spaces before:
   a. A parenthesis following a sentence
   b. An opening quotation mark that follows a sentence
7. There is one space after:
   a. An abbreviation within a sentence
   b. A comma
   c. A semicolon
   d. A closing parenthesis or bracket used within a sentence
   e. An apostrophe that ends a word within a sentence
   f. An asterisk following a word within a sentence
8. There are two spaces after:
   a. A period that ends a sentence
   b. A period used for enumeration
   c. A closing quotation mark that ends a sentence
   d. A question mark that ends a sentence
   e. An exclamation point that ends a sentence
   f. An asterisk at the end of a sentence
   g. A colon within a sentence
   h. Parentheses or brackets that enclose complete sentences
   i. A dash that ends an abrupt statement

● **2-3** Indicate the correct number of spaces for each item by drawing a circle around the appropriate number. (5 points each correct item)

Number of Spaces

1. There should be _____ space(s) after a period that ends a sentence.

   1. 0 1 2

2. There should be _____ space(s) before a comma.

   2. 0 1 2

3. There should be _____ space(s) between single and double quotation marks.

   3. 0 1 2

4. There should be _____ space(s) before and after an apostrophe within a word.

   4. 0 1 2

5. There should be _____ space(s) after an apostrophe if it is at the end of a word but within a sentence.

   5. 0 1 2

6. There should be _____ space(s) before a colon.

   6. 0 1 2

7. There should be _____ space(s) after a decimal point within a number.

   7. 0 1 2

8. There should be _____ space(s) after commas in a number.

   8. 0 1 2

9. There should be _____ space(s) after an abbreviation within the sentence.

   9. 0 1 2

10. There is no space before a semicolon, but there should be _____ space(s) after a semicolon.

    10. 0 1 2

11. There is no space before a diagonal, and there should be _____ space(s) after a diagonal.

    11. 0 1 2

Number of
Spaces

12. There should be _____ space(s) after a period following a number or letter used for enumeration.

12. 0 1 2

13. After a comma, there should be _____ space(s) (unless there is a closing quotation mark immediately following the comma).

13. 0 1 2

14. There should be _____ space(s) following a quotation mark that ends a sentence.

14. 0 1 2

15. There is no space before an asterisk, but there should be _____ space(s) after an asterisk at the end of a sentence.

15. 0 1 2

16. There should be _____ space(s) after an asterisk within a sentence.

16. 0 1 2

17. There should be _____ space(s) before an opening parenthesis or bracket that encloses parenthetic material within a sentence.

17. 0 1 2

18. There should be _____ space(s) before an opening parenthesis or bracket that encloses material that follows a sentence.

18. 0 1 2

19. When using opening quotation marks, there is no space after, but there should be _____ space(s) before when the quotation begins a sentence or follows a colon.

19. 0 1 2

20. When using closing quotation marks, there is no space before the mark, but there should be _____ space(s) after when the quotation ends a sentence.

20. 0 1 2

PROOFREADERS' MARKS FOR ADDING AND DELETING SPACE

To indicate that a space should be added or deleted, use these marks:

To add space

On the#desk

To close space

On the de⁀sk

To leave one space

On⁀ the desk

To show that a paragraph should be indented the usual five spaces, use the symbol shown in this example:

5 On April 1, we will begin our sales
campaign. Sales representatives will
receive bonus points for each new account.

● **2-4** Proofread the following items to find spacing errors. Mark each error with the appropriate proofreaders' mark. (10 points each corrected item)

1. Inthe files

2. for each ac count

3. all new   employees

4. 22. 357

5. 23, 085

6. (612) 555 - 8176

7. December 9,1968

8. Don' t give him the report.

9. Send me $10 (check or money order) within 30 days.

10. The article, "Upward Mobiles, " was in yesterday's paper.

● **2-5** Proofread the following paragraphs to find ten spacing errors. Correct each error with the appropriate proofreaders' mark. (10 points each corrected error)

Paragraph 1

Our plant began operation July 1,1985,at its new location on Holden Street. Our success--due totally to the efforts of our dedicated employees--has exceeded that of our biggest competition.

Paragraph 2

The supervisor made this statement: " Continued ab-sences will not be tolerated; a word to the wise shouldbe sufficient!"

Paragraph 3

Several ofour employees will receive service awards at our retirement banquet next week: Mrs.Martha Landers (25 years), Mr. Ted Salina (20 years),and Ms. Deborah Trexler (15 years).

● **2-6** The first memo on the next page is correct; the second one is not. Compare them carefully. Use revision symbols to correct transpositions, spacing errors, omissions, and repetitions. (10 points each corrected error)

MEMORANDUM

Date   March 30, 1987

To   Bill Martina, Office Manager

From   Celia Dominique, President

Subject Power Interruption

The power company has just notified us that our electricity will be off Saturday morning between 8:30 and 10:30. This interruption is necessary to repair the damage done by the recent ice storm.

Saturday will be a convenient time because we are closed. However, please make whatever power backup arrangements are necessary to keep our computer operating. Also, post a notice about the power interruption on each entrance in case some employees plan to be in the building on Saturday.

                              CD

MEMORANDUM

Date   March 30, 1978

To   Bill Martin, Office Manager

From   Celia Dominique, President

Subject Power Interruption

The power company has just notified us that our electricity will be off Saturday morning between 8:03 and 10:30. This interruption is necessary to repair   the damage done by teh recent ice storm.

Saturday will be a convenient time because we are closed. However, please make what ever power backup arrangements are are necessary to keep our computer operating. Also,post a notice about the power interruption on each entrance incase some employees plan to be the in building on Saturday.

                              CD

● **2-7** Read and compare the following pairs of paragraphs. In each pair, the first paragraph is correct. Proofread the second paragraph, using the appropriate proofreaders' marks to correct spacing, omissions, repetitions, transpositions, and paragraph indentions. (10 points each correct revision)

Paragraph 1

> Last year you supplied the gifts for our company field day. We were pleased with your selection and with your service. Will you give us your recommendations for this year's field day? We need gifts totaling $1600. The first prize should range from $450 to $500. The second, third, and fourth prizes should be in the $150 to $350 range. We would also like 20 fifth prizes in the $15 to $25 range.

Last year you supplied the gifts for our company field day. We were pleased with your selection and with your service. Will you give us your recommendations for this year's field day? We need 24 gifts totaling $1600. The first prize should range from $450 to $500. The second, third,and fourth prizes should be in the $150 to $350 range. We would also like 20 fifth prizes in the $15 to $25 range.

Paragraph 2

> We are eager to supply gifts for your company field day. The following 24 gifts fit the price ranges you listed:

Quantity	Description	Price	Total
1	Microwave oven	$460	$ 460
1	Portable television (color)	350	350
1	Stereo console	225	225
1	Stereo tape deck	165	165
5	Cassette recorder	25	125
5	Toaster oven	20	100
5	Electric blanket	20	100
5	Electric frying pan	15	75
	Total		$1600

We are eager to supply gifts for you company field day. The following 24

gifts fit the price ranges you listed:

Quantity	Description	Price	Total
1	Microwave oven	$460	$ 460
1	Portable television (color)	350	350
1	Stereo console	225	225
1	Stereo tape deck	165	165
5	Cassette recorder	25	125
5	Toaster ovenn	20	100
5	Electric blanket	20	100
5	Electric frying pan	15	75
	Total		$1600

Paragraph 3

Thank you for your prompt reply to our request for gift-selection recommendations. Our committee unanimously approved the selection. Use our purchase order 8945, and deliver the gifts to our Personnel Department by July 1. Please call me if you need further information.

Thankyou for your prompt reply to our request for gift-selection recommendations. Our committee unanimously approved the selection. Use our purchase order 9845, and deliver the gifts to our Personnel Department by July 1. Please call me if you need further information.

Paragraph 4

Please let me know by tomorrow afternoon how the plans are progressing for the company field day. Last year's field day was a tremendous success, and this year's should be even better. Stay within our $12,000 budget.

Please let me know by tomorrow afternoon how the plans are progressing for the company feild day. Last year's feild day was tremendous success, and this year's should be even better. Stay within our $12,000 budget.

Paragraph 5

The prizes for this year's field day are as follows:

First prize	Microwave oven
Second prize	Portable television (color)
Third prize	Stereo console
Fourth prize	Stereo tape deck
Fifth prizes	Cassette recorders (5)
	Toaster ovens (5)
	Electric blankets (5)
	Electric frying pans (5)

The prizes for for this year's field day areas follows:

First prize	Microwave oven
Second prize	Portable television (color)
Third prize	Stereo console
Fourth prize	Stereo tape deck
Fifth prizes	Cassette recorders (5)
	Toaster ovens (5)
	Toaster ovens (5)
	Electric blankets (5)
	Electric frying pans (5)

● **2-8** The letter below is correct; the one on the facing page is *not.* Compare them carefully, one line at a time. Use proofreaders' marks to correct transposition errors in words and figures, spacing errors, and omission and repetition errors. For each line that is correct, place a check mark (✔) in the space provided. For each line that has an error, place an *x* in the space. (5 points each check mark or corrected error)

WALL DECORATIONS, INC.
POST OFFICE BOX 7125
ALBUQUERQUE, NEW MEXICO 87104
(505) 555-8194

November 13, 1987

Mr. Carlos D. Manos, President
Manos Paint and Supply Company
Post Office Box 2137
Albuquerque, NM 87104

Dear Mr. Manos:

    Thank you for your letter asking for more information about our new wallpaper line. We appreciate the opportunity to introduce you to the newest designs, quality supplies, and prompt, courteous service.

    Our sales representative for your area, Terry Spielberg, will call you this week to arrange an appointment to show you styles and colors that will seem to sell themselves to your customers. Terry will also bring samples of supplies and tools needed in wallpaper applications.

    Your copy of our latest catalog is enclosed. If I can be of any further help, please call me.

               Very truly yours,

               WALL DECORATIONS, INC.

               Ellen N. Burnette

js
Enclosure

WALL DECORATIONS, INC.

POST OFFICE BOX 7125
ALBUQUERQUE, NEW MEXICO 87104
(505) 555-8194

✔/x

November 13, 1987   1. _____

Mr. Carlos D. Manos, President   2. _____
Manos Paint and Supply Company   3. _____
Post Office Box 2173   4. _____
Albuquerque,NM 87104   5. _____

Dear Mr. Manos: 6. _____

   Thank you for your letter asking for more information about our   7. _____
new wallpaper line. We appreciate the opportunity to introduce you to   8. _____
the newest designs, quality supplies, and prompt courteous service.   9. _____

Our sales representative for your area, Terry Spielberg, will call   10. _____
you this week to arrange an appointment to show you styles and colors   11. _____
that will seem to sell them selves to your customers. Terry will also   12. _____
bring samples of supplies and tools needed in wallpaper applications.   13. _____

   Your copy of our latest catalog is enclosed. If I be can of any   14. _____
any further help, please call me.   15. _____

                        Very truly yours,   16. _____

                        WALL DECORATIONS, INC.   17. _____

                        Ellen N. Burnette   18. _____

js   19. _____
Enclosure   20. _____

● **2-9** The first letter is correct; the one on the facing page is *not*. Compare them carefully, one line at a time. Use proofreaders' marks to correct transposition errors in words and figures, spacing errors, and omission and repetition errors. For each line that is correct, place a check mark (✓) in the space provided. For each line that has an error, place an x in the space. (5 points each check mark or corrected error)

COSTUMES & THEATRICAL SUPPLIES

BROADWAY SPECIALTIES Ltd.

PEACHTREE INDUSTRIAL PARK   POST OFFICE BOX 745
NORCROSS, GEORGIA 30091   (404) 555-4862

March 30, 1986

Mrs. Angelina Beckwith
City Theater Productions
212 West Oglethorpe Boulevard
Athens, Georgia 31701

Dear Mrs. Beckwith:

Thank you for ordering your theatrical costumes from us. Your cast will be pleased with the realism that our designers and staff have spent many hours producing.

You may rent the costumes for <u>The King and I</u> for $25 each. They must be returned within 12 days. We can alter and ship the costumes within two weeks after we get the measurements of your cast. If you prefer to do the alterations, we can ship the costumes the same day you request them.

You asked about our makeup service. We will be happy to send our representative to your dress rehearsal and/or your opening night. This service (which includes the makeup) will cost $150 per night.

Please let me know how we can best serve your needs.

Yours very truly,

Gail L. French
Director of Costume Services

jk

COSTUMES & THEATRICAL SUPPLIES

BROADWAY SPECIALTIES LTD.

PEACHTREE INDUSTRIAL PARK   POST OFFICE BOX 745
NORCROSS, GEORGIA 30091   (404) 555-4862

✔ / x

March 30, 1986

1. _____

Mrs. Angelina Beckwith
City Theater Productions
212 West Oglethorpe Boulevard
Athens, Georgia 31701

2. _____
3. _____
4. _____
5. _____

Dear Mrs. Beckwith:

6. _____

Thank you for ordering your theatrical costumes from us. Your cast wil11
be pleased with the realism that our designers and staff have spent
many hours producing.

7. _____
8. _____
9. _____

You may rent the costumes for The King and I for $25 each. They must be
returned within 21 days. We can alter and ship the costumes witin two
weeks after we get the measurements of your cast. If you prefer to do
the alterations, we can ship the costumes the same day you request them.

10. _____
11. _____
12. _____
13. _____

You asked about our makeup service. We will be happy to send our
representative to your dress rehearsal and / or your opening night. This
service (which includes the makeup) will cost $150 per per night.

14. _____
15. _____
16. _____

Please let me know how wecan best serve your needs.

17. _____

Yours very truly,

18. _____

Gail L. French
Director of Costume Services

19. _____

jk

20. _____

Proofreading Review

Demonstrate what you have learned by completing the following exercises. Exercise 2-A includes additional practice based on this chapter. Exercise 2-B is cumulative; it includes principles covered both in Chapters 1 and 2.

● **2-A** There are two parts to Exercise 2-A. (5 points each correct answer)
In questions 1–15, two of the three items listed are identical; one is different. For each question, identify the column with the different item by writing *A, B,* or *C* in the space provided.

	A	B	C	
1.	248-72-1948	248-72-1948	248-72-9148	1. _____
2.	246-12-4829	246-12-4829	264-12-4829	2. _____
3.	365-32-4825	365-23-4825	365-32-4825	3. _____
4.	449-87-6135	449-78-6135	449-78-6135	4. _____
5.	322-43-3324	322-43-3342	322-43-3324	5. _____
6.	233-86-4326	233-86-3426	233-86-3426	6. _____
7.	(503) 423-7151	(503) 423-7151	(503) 243-7151	7. _____
8.	(217) 572-5959	(217) 572-5995	(217) 572-5995	8. _____
9.	(405 463-2475	(405) 463-2475	(405) 463-2475	9. _____
10.	(219) 699-4131	(219) 699-4311	(219) 699-4131	10. _____
11.	your convenience	your conveneince	your convenience	11. _____
12.	at your request	at your request	at your requesst	12. _____
13.	determining	determing	determining	13. _____
14.	in the book	in the book	the in book	14. _____
15	final annalysis	final analysis	final analysis	15. _____

In questions 16–20, one item in each pair is correctly spaced. Circle the item, *a* or *b,* that is correct.

16. a. Your application has been received and
      reviewed.Please call me to arrange an interview.
    b. Your application has been received and
      reviewed. Please call me to arrange an interview.
17. a. "Your new word processor," said the sales
      representative, "will improve office productivity."
    b. "Your new word processor,"said the sales
      representative, "will improve office productivity."
18. a. Use memos to communicate within the company; use
      letters outside the company.
    b. Use memos to communicate within the company;use
      letters outside the company.
19. a. He bought these supplies: continuous feed paper,
      labels, and ribbons.
    b. He bought these supplies: continuous feed paper,
      labels, and ribbons.
20. a. We have 10, 235 employees in our five branches.
    b. We have 10,235 employees in our five branches.

● **2-B** Below and on the next page are the business cards of some of the companies with which your company corresponds regularly. You asked your assistant to type cards that fit into your address and telephone file for each of these businesses. The following information should be on each file card:

Name of individual and title (if given)　　　Mailing address
Company name　　　　　　　　　　　　　　　Phone number

Proofread each file card below and on the next page to make sure it is accurate. If a file card is correct, place a check mark (√) in the space provided in the lower right-hand corner. If a file card has one or more errors, correct each error using the appropriate proofreaders' mark. Refer to the list of proofreaders' marks on the inside back cover. (5 points each appropriate check mark and each corrected error)

Grogan's
Gas and Service

Ben Grogan, *Owner and Operator*

Route 6 • Akron, OH 44313　　　*(216) 555-8864*

---

(216) 555-9302

First Commerce Bank

Alma D. Quinten,
Vice President

Post Office Box 3500 • Akron, OH 44310

AKRON TOOL and GEAR Company

Hansen S. Cunningham,
Sales Representative

Post Office Box 4445 • Akron, OH 44321 • (216) 555-3478

DAILY NEWS and **Observer**

Linda L. Langley
Advertising Manager

2219 East Talbot Place • Akron, OH 43223
(216) 555-7695

HIGHTOWER
Manufacturing Company

Ina Jane Bergman, *Controller*

2234 Freedom Avenue • Akron, OH 44310 • (216) 555-9887

---

(216) 555-6785

Baxters Refrigeration Company

2385 Alma Avenue • Akron, OH 44319

Arnold Bronson, *Serviceman*

Akron Tool and Gear Company　　　1
Post Office Box 4445
Akron, OH 44321

Hansen S. Cunningham
Sales Representative

Phone:　(216) 555-3478　　　　　—

Baxters Refrigeration Company　　2
2385 Avenue
Akron, OH 44319

Arnold Bronson
Serviceman

Phone:　(216) 555-6785　　　　　—

Daily News and Observer　　　　3
2219 East Talbot Place
Akron, OH 43223

Linda L. Langley
Advertising Manager

Phone:　(216) 555-7695　　　　　—

First Commerce Bank　　　　　　4
Post Office Box 350
Akron, OH 44310

Alma D. Quinten
Vice President

Phone:　(216) 555-9302　　　　　—

Grogan's Gasand Service　　　　5
Route 6
Akorn, OH 44313

Ben Grogan, Owner and Operator

Phone:　(216) 555-8864　　　　　—

Hightower Manufacturing Company　6
2243 Freedom Avenue
Akron, HO 44310

Ina Jane Bergman
Controller

Phone:　(216) 555-9887　　　　　—

(continued)

(continued)

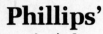

Phillips'

Jewelry Store

Edna Phillips, *Senior Accountant*

Cromwell Terrace • Akron, OH 44313   (216) 555-9878

Syer's

Department Store

Jamin F. Parks, *Manager*

Post Office Box 9003 • Akron, OH 44305 • (216) 555-3485

Stantons Inn

One Stanton Drive
Akron, OH 44314

Mable Oglesby, *Manager*

(216) 555-9788

Freida Stanton,
Marketing Manager

Johnson Office Supply, Inc.

443 Douglas Drive
Columbus, OH 43230

(614) 555-8095

Kirk's

Surf-N-Turf

Anthony Kirk, Owner

Andover Lane • Akron, OH 44312 • (216) 555-5783

Sweeney's Music Store

Hickory Creek Mall

Edna Sweeney,
Sales Representative

2323 Coleman Avenue
Akron, OH 44312   (216) 555-5789

```
Johnson Office Supplies, Inc.        7
443 Doglas Drive
Columbus, OH 43230

Freida Stanton
Marketing Manager

Phone:  (614) 555-8095              ___
```

```
Kirk's Surf-N-Turf                   8
Andower Lane
Akron, OH 44312

Anthony Kirk, Owner

Phone:  (216) 555-5783             ___
```

```
Philips' Jewelery Store              9
Cromwell Terrace
Akron, OH 44313

Edna Phillips, Accountant

Phone:  (216) 555-9878             ___
```

```
Stanton's Inn                       10
One Stanton Drive
Akron, OH 44314

Mable Oglesby, Manager

Phone:  (216) 555-9878             ___
```

```
Sweeney's Music Store               11
Hickory Creek Mall
2323 Colman Avenue
Akron, OH 44212

Edna Sweeney
Sales Representative

Phone:  (216) 555-5789             ___
```

```
Syer's Department Store             12
Post Office Box 9003
Akron, OH

Jamin F. Parks, Manager

Phone:  (216) 555-3458             ___
```

3.

Proofreaders' Marks

Routine letters, memos, and reports are usually dictated and transcribed with little need for revision. However, not all letters, memos, and reports are routine. Many business communications—especially those that are long and complicated—require careful thought and careful wording of the message. For these nonroutine situations, the writer will usually prepare a rough draft (handwritten, typewritten, or printed) and revise it one or more times. When all the revisions have been made, the final copy is typed or printed.

In revising the draft copy, the writer must mark any changes or corrections in a standard way—in a way that all keyboard operators and all business writers can understand. The proofreaders' marks shown on the inside back cover of this book are the ones most frequently used to make corrections.

In Chapters 1 and 2, you learned to use some of the proofreaders' marks (also called revision symbols); in Chapter 3, you will learn to use all of the symbols you must know to mark corrections on your job.

Proofreading and Automated Equipment

Technology offers new capabilities. Thus, new or once infrequently used symbols deserve our attention. For example, automated equipment lets the operator insert, delete, or move a block of text. A block of text can be a phrase, a paragraph, or a longer segment, such as a page. You can identify a block by marking the beginning and end and labeling it with an alphabetic character. The following example shows how to identify a block and then delete it using the delete symbol ( ).

The sales meeting will be held/early in the morning/on Monday, February 5, at 8 a.m., in our conference room.

Here is the sentence correctly printed:

The sales meeting will be held on Monday, February 5, at 8 a.m., in our conference room.

Many printers now offer boldface printing. Drawing a wavy line under a word or under several words would signal the keyboard operator to use boldface printing. The wavy line under SOFTWARE CREATIVITY tells the operator to print those words in boldface.

31

Our theme is SOFTWARE CREATIVITY.

Here is the sentence showing the boldface printing:

Our theme is **SOFTWARE CREATIVITY**.

Look at the following letter and the one on the facing page. They illustrate the use of proofreaders' marks. The first letter is a typed rough draft with changes and corrections indicated. The second letter is the final copy with the changes and corrections made. Look at each handwritten change in the first letter, and then see how the change was handled in the final copy. Refer to the inside back cover for the meaning of symbols any time you need clarification.

August 1, 1987 ⟶

Ms. Celia Henshaw, PRESIDENT
Software Designs, Inc.
2116 Bedford Court
Wichita, KS   67207

Dear Ms. Henshaw:

    Next month, our company is sponsoring a computer fair (the/at
merchandise mart in Kansas City, Kansas|merchandise mart in
Kansas City, Kansas. This year's theme is|SOFTWARE CREATIVITY|]Ⓑ[
and the dates of the fair will be (Sept.) 7 to 11. This topic
ds ⎡ has stimulated alot of interest in the software market.
   ⎣   We would like very much for you to display some of your
software and and your most recent book, Software Selection.
Also, we would like you to be available for ① or ② hours each
day to graph copies of your book for customers.

    We look forward to hearing from you.| move
                                                               Ⓒ

5 At your earliest convenience, please let us no if our visitors
will have the privilege of meeting you and seeing your Software
designs. Sam oliver, who handles the staffing of booths, says
that his up-to-date report indicates that only a few boooths
are available.

> Ⓒ   Sincerely yours,

                             Johnsie K. Sumner,
                             (Chairman) Special Projects Committee

hb

Post Office Box 3290
Kansas City, KS 67207-3290
(913) 555-4390

August 1, 1987

Ms. Celia Henshaw, President
Software Designs, Inc.
2116 Bedford Court
Wichita, KS 67207

Dear Ms. Henshaw:

Next month, our company is sponsoring a computer fair at the merchandise mart in Kansas City, Kansas. This year's theme is

SOFTWARE CREATIVITY

and the dates of the fair will be September 7 to 14. This topic has stimulated a lot of interest in the software market.

We would like very much for you to display some of your software and your most recent book, SOFTWARE SELECTION. Also, we would like you to be available for one or two hours each day to autograph your book for customers.

At your earliest convenience, please let us know if our visitors will have the privilege of meeting you and seeing your software designs. Sam Oliver, who handles the staffing of booths, says that his up-to-date report indicates that only a few booths are available.

We look forward to hearing from you.

Sincerely yours,

Johnsie K. Sumner, Chairman
Special Projects Committee

hb

▼▼ Proofreading Pointers

▼ Be alert as you work. Not making errors is better than finding and correcting errors later.

▼ Be sure of your instructions. When in doubt, ask the appropriate person.

▼ Use an easy-to-follow, consistent set of proofreaders' marks.

▼ To avoid having proofreaders' marks overlooked, use a bright-colored pen to mark changes or corrections.

● **3-1** In each of the following items, make the corrections indicated by the proofreaders' marks. Write the entire corrected sentence in the space provided. (5 points each corrected revision)

1. Tom Baxter plans open his own business next spring.

   _____

   _____

2. Our copy machine produces transparencies for for overhead projectors.

   _____

   _____

3. Approximately three to ⑤ employees will qualify for bonuses.

   _____

   _____

4. Send your application to the personnel Department by Oct. 15.

   _____

   _____

5. Most of our sales staff recieve on the job training.

   _____

   _____

6. Our computer programmers know Basic, Fortran, and Cobol.

   _____

   _____

7. We need a computer consultant to help us determine our needs.

   _____

   _____

8. We plan to turn to miami on Tuesday, April 5.

   _____

   _____

9. Her book, Reaching Your Goals, willbe published next month.

   _____

   _____

10. Place the ad in our local news paper for ~~four~~ *six* days.

_____

_____

● **3-2**   Read and compare the following pairs of paragraphs.

In each pair, the first paragraph—with all its handwritten corrections—is correct. The second paragraph is a retyped version of the first paragraph. In retyping the first paragraph, did the typist follow the proofreaders' marks accurately?

Proofread the second paragraph carefully, line by line to make sure that the typist made the corrections indicated in the first paragraph and did not introduce any errors. Correct any error by using the appropriate proofreaders' mark, and then mark *x* on the line provided. If a line has no error, place a check mark (✔) on the line provided. (5 points each line correctly marked)

Paragraph 1

On June 28, 1980, the committee met to discuss prizes for the department with the best cost-reduction idea for the quarter ending June 30, 1980. First prize will be a night on the town, including a baseball game, dinner, dancing, and *the* next day off with pay.

On June 28, 1980, the committee met to discuss _____
prizes for the department with the best cost-reduction _____
idea for the quarter ending June 30, 1980. First _____
prize will be a night on the town, including a baseball _____
game, dinner, dancing, and the next day off with pay. _____

Paragraph 2

Second-place winners will *at*tend a dinner-theater production of the well-known musical The Sound of Music. The Patriot Players of ~~of~~ New York City will present this play, using some of the original broadway cast.

Second-place winners will attend a dinner— _____
theater production of the well known musical _____
The Sound of Music. The Patriot Players of _____
New York City will present this play, using some _____
of the original Broadway cast. _____

Paragraph 3

Third-place winners will receive a
$10 gift certificate for dinner (the/at)
Rotesta Disco and Steak House. If the winner
prefers, a check for $10 may be given in lieu
of the gift certificate.

Third-place winners will receive a   ____
$10 gift certificate for dinner that   ____
Rotesta Disco and Steak House. If the winner   ____
prefers, check for $10 may be given in lieu   ____
of the gift certificate.   ____

Paragraph 4

The Data Processing Department is ahead
in the cost-reduction contest and will probably
claim first place; however, the Shipping (Dept.)
is running a close second place place. The staff in
the purchasing Department is trying for third place.

The Data Processing Department is ahead   ____
in the cost-reduction contest and will probably   ____
claim first place. However, the Shipping Department   ____
is running a close second place. The staff in   ____
the purchasing department is trying for third place.   ____

● **3-3** In each of the following pairs, item b is correct while item a contains
at least one error. Compare a with b and then make the corrections in item a.
Be sure to use the appropriate proofreaders' marks. (10 points each sentence
correctly marked)

1. a. Two out of 3 employees are taking advantage of our dental and health insurance.
   b. Two out of three employees are taking advantage of our dental and health insurance.
2. a. Lester Oneida will attend the Fall conference on management techniques.
   b. Lester Oneida will attend the fall conference on management techniques.
3. a. Mr. and Mrs Chang are attending night classes at Claxton community College.
   b. Mr. and Mrs. Chang are attending night classes at Claxton Community College.
4. a. Last month, we had ZERO defects in our production.
   b. Last month, we had **ZERO** defects in our production.
5. a. We improved quality with out increasing defect the in products shipped.
   b. We improved quality without increasing defects in the products shipped.
6. a. Information systems give management up to date information for decision making.
   b. Information systems give management up-to-date information for decision making.

7. a. Your reccommendation were accepted by the advisory committee.

   b. Your recommendations were accepted by the advisory committee.

8. a. Bills vacation request was received January 13.

   b. Bill's vacation request was received January 31.

9. a. "You are doing a great job, the supervisor told Kathryn during her performance appraisal.

   b. "You are doing a great job," the supervisor told Kathryn during her performance appraisal.

10. a. The report revealed shocking statisstisticss.

    b. The report revealed some shocking statistics.

Proofreading From Handwritten Drafts

Authorities estimate that as much as 70 percent of information put into automated systems originates from handwritten drafts. The next few exercises will give you practice in comparing handwritten drafts with typed copy.

● **3-4** A rough draft may be handwritten before it is typed. Proofread the following pairs of handwritten and typed copy. Is the copy in Column B the same as the copy in column A? If it is, write *yes* in the space provided. If it is not, write *no* in the space. (10 points for each correct item)

A	B	Yes/No?
1. Invoice 1432	Invvoice 1432	1. _____
2. $11,943.05	$11,934.05	2. _____
3. 221-72-4433	221-72-4433	3. _____
4. Mrs. Bethany Winslow	Mrs. Bethany Winslow	4. _____
5. 12-25-87	12-25-87	5. _____
6. 74134-2166	71434-2166	6. _____
7. Wilmington, DE 19810	Wilmington, DL 19810	7. _____
8. August 25, 1919	August 25, 1919	8. _____
9. 10:20 p.m.	10:20 a.m.	9. _____
10. (503) 654-3820	(503) 654-3820	10. _____

● **3-5** Compare the handwritten sentence with the typewritten sentence. If they are the same, write *yes* in the space provided. If they are different, write *no* in the space. (10 points for each correct item)

Yes/No?

1. *Business writers often like to compose letters and memorandums using a word processor.*

   Business writers often like to compose letters and
   and memorandums using a word processor.   1. _____

2. *Automation has opened new career paths for those employed in office occupations.*

   Automation has opened new career path for those employed in office occupations.   2. _____

3. *Many suburban communities have modern office parks that are designed to house several different administrative complexes.*

Many suburban communities have modern office parks that are designed to house different administrative.

3. _____

4. *The staff of modern offices must possess a combination of skills, aptitudes, and talents.*

The staff of modern offices must possess a combination of skills, aptitudes, and talents.

4. _____

5. *Some computers have software packages that simplify the making of graphs.*

Some computers have software packages that simplify the making of grapfs.

5. _____

6. *Please check the price for our stationery printed on continuous feed computer paper.*

Please check the price for our stationary printed on continuous feed computer paper.

6. _____

7. *Preparation is the key to a successful job interview.*

Preparation is teh key to a successful job interview.

7. _____

8. *An effective manager is an expert in human relations.*

An effective manager is an expert in human relations.

8. _____

9. *Our company pays for each employee's health, dental, and life insurance coverage.*

Our company pays for each employees health, dental, and life insurance coverage.

9. _____

10. *Your company has experienced phenomenal growth during the last ten years.*

Your company has experienced phenomenal growth during the last ten years.

10. _____

● **3-6** Compare the following pairs of paragraphs to see if the typewritten paragraph is the same as the handwritten paragraph. Using the appropriate proofreaders' marks, indicate in the typewritten paragraph any changes that should be made to make it like the handwritten paragraph. (10 points each difference correctly marked)

Paragraph 1

Five applicants for the position of assistant general manager will be arriving Monday about 6 p.m. Our first contact with them will be at dinner, which will be served in our hotel's private dining room.

Five applicants for the position of assistant manager will be
arriving Monday about 6 a.m. Our first contact with them will be at
dinner, which will be served in our hotel's private dinning room.

Paragraph 2

Room reservations have been made for each
applicant. However, please see that these items are
placed in the rooms: a newspaper, a city map, and
a copy of the book, Houston -- A Great Place to Live.
Also, have each room inspected by the head
housekeeper to assure that everything is in the
best possible order.

Room reservations have been made for each applicant. However, please
see than these items are placed in the rooms: a newspaper, a city map,
and a copy of the book, Houston--A Great Place to Live. Also, have each
room inspected by the head housekeeper ot assure that everything is in
the best possible order.

Paragraph 3

We are trying to attract the most qualified
person with the greatest potential for increasing
our revenues. All five applicants have strong
human relations, management, and marketing
backgrounds.

We are trying to attract the most qualified person with the
greatest potential for increasing out revenues. All five applicants
have strong human relations management, and Marketing backgrounds.

● **3-7** Compare the handwritten memorandum below with the typewritten memorandum on the next page. The handwritten draft is correct. Use the appropriate proofreaders' marks to mark corrections in the typewritten copy. (20 points each correction)

Memorandum

Date: April 19, 1987

To: Office Personnel

From: Bernard Franklin

Subject: Photocopying Machine

Beginning immediately, the charge for personal copies will increase from 5 to 10 cents. This adjustment is necessary because of rising maintenance and supply costs.

Thank you for your cooperation. We are glad that we can provide this convenience for you.

BF

MEMORANDUM

Date: April 19, 1987

To: Office Personnel

From: Bernard Franklin

Subject: Photocopying Machine

Beginning immediately, the charge for personal copies will increase from 5 to 10 cent. This adjustment is necessary because of rising maintainance and supply costs.

Thankyou for our cooperation. We are glad that we can provide this convenience for you.

                        FB

Proofreading Review

● **3-A** Compare the handwritten draft below with the final printed copy on the next page. Use proofreaders' marks on the printed copy to mark changes that were indicated on the handwritten draft but not correctly made on the final copy.

September 15, 19--

Dr. Manuel R. Mendosa
Children's Clinic
Post Office Box 10948
Amarillo, TX 79106

Dear Dr. Mendosa:

Thank you for your recent order of furniture to be used in your
pediatric practice. You have selected attractive, durable furnishings
that will be appropriate and comfortable for those who visit your
offices.

I will personally be with the crew while they are decorating your
offices. Please let me know if you want any last-minute changes. | move A

As requested, your furniture will be delivered by 8:30 a.m., Saturday,
morning, Sept. 21. We will remove your old items and place your new
furnishings according to the floor plan mailed to you previously.

Your agreement with us to have your new office decor featured in the
December issue of The Professional Office will give you a 10% discount
from the original price we quoted. The article will give us some good
publicity.

A

Sincerely,

C. A. Dennis
Account Executive

gh

Professional Interiors, Inc.
Post Office Box 10247
Amarillo, Texas 79106
(806) 555-8179

September 15, 19--

Dr. Manuel R. Mendosa
Children's Clinic
Post Office Box 10984
Amarillo, TX 79106

Dear Dr. Mendosa:

Thank you for your recent order of furniture to be used in your practice. You have selected attractive, durable furnishings that will be appropriate and comfortable for those who visit your offices.

I will personally be with the crew while they are decorating your offices. Please let me know if you want any last-minute changes.

As requested, your furniture will be delivered by 8:30 a.m., Saturday, Sept. 21. We will remove your old items and place your new furnishings according to the floor plan mailed to you previously.

Your agreement with us to have your new office decor featured in the December issue of The Professional Office will give you a 10 percent discount from the original price we quoted. The article will give us some good publicity.

I will personally be with the crew while they are decorating your offices. Please let me know if you want any last-minute changes.

                              Sincerely,

                              C. A. Dennis
                              Account Executive

gh

● **3-B** During lunch, the receptionist took the four messages below for your supervisor, Alice Cranshaw. When Ms. Cranshaw is away from the office for several days, she prefers a printed list of her messages rather than individual message slips. Assuming that the telephone message slips are correct, mark any needed changes in the printed list on the next page which was keyboarded by your secretary. Accuracy is important in all communications—no matter how informal.

---

to _Alice Cranshaw_   date _9/15/--_   time _12:05_

while you were out...

m _Judd Yezek_
co _City Free Service_
tel _(401) 335-8164_
   area code   number   extension

- [ ] telephoned
- [ ] please call
- [ ] will call again
- [✓] returned your call
- [ ] urgent

- [ ] called to see you
- [ ] wants to see you

message _He has the estimate you requested on removing the trees damaged during the ice storm. Cost will be $918._
        by _Dana Montief_

---

to _Alice Cranshaw_   date _9/15/--_   time _12:35_

while you were out...

ms. _Angelina Matsuura_
co _None_
tel _(401) 335-8165_
   area code   number   extension

- [✓] telephoned
- [✓] please call
- [ ] will call again
- [ ] returned your call
- [ ] urgent

- [ ] called to see you
- [ ] wants to see you

message _She wants to talk with you about a personal matter._
        by _Dana Montief_

---

to _Alice Cranshaw_   date _9/15/--_   time _12:40_

while you were out...

mr. _Edgar Malpeli_
co _Malpeli and Associates_
tel _(401) 335- 9981_
   area code   number   extension

- [✓] telephoned
- [✓] please call
- [ ] will call again
- [ ] returned your call
- [ ] urgent

- [ ] called to see you
- [ ] wants to see you

message _He wants to talk with you about office equipment._
        by _Dana Montief_

---

to _Alice Cranshaw_   date _9/15/--_   time _12:45_

while you were out...

ms. _Jane Kraft_
co _J&K Leasing_
tel _(401) 335-2247_
   area code   number   extension

- [✓] telephoned
- [✓] please call
- [ ] will call again
- [ ] returned your call
- [ ] urgent

- [ ] called to see you
- [ ] wants to see you

message _She will bring your new car whenever you want it._
        by _Dana Montief_

Messages for
ALICE CRANSHAW
September 15, 19--

These messages were taken by Dana Montief.

Mr. Judd Yesek
City Tree Service
(401) 335-8164

Returned Your Call

Message: He has the estimate you requested on removing the trees
damaged during the ice storm. The cost will be $198.

Time: 12:05

Ms. Angelina Matsura
No company name given
(401) 335-8165

Telephoned
Please Call

Message: She wants to talk with you about a personal matter.

Time: 12:35

Mr. Edgar Malpeli
Malpeli and Associates
(401) 335-9981

Telephoned
Please Call

Message: He wants to talk with you about office equipment.

Time: 12:40

Ms. Jane Kraft
J & K Leasing
(401) 335-2247

Telephoned
Please Call

Message: She will bring your new car whenever you want it.

Time: 12:45

Number Alertness

Proofreading Numbers

Letters, memos, invoices, orders, and most other business communications often include numbers. Numbers are used for dates, measurements, dollar amounts, quantities, sizes, and so on. It is particularly important for the writer to proofread numbers carefully because the reader has no way of knowing that 756 feet should really be 765 feet or that 34.6 percent should really be 43.6 percent. The writer must check each numeral to make sure it is accurate.

To proofread numbers, you must concentrate carefully on each number as you check it.

▼▼ Proofreading Pointers

▼ Divide long numbers of four or more digits into groups. For example, when proofreading a column of dollar figures, read $17,435.79 as follows: "seventeen/ four-three-five/point-seven-nine."

▼ When reading columns of numbers, use a 3 by 5 card to keep your place so that your eyes won't jump from one number to another.

▼ When proofreading long columns of numbers, have one person read the numbers from the original copy while a second person checks that the numbers have been accurately recorded on the final copy.

Style for Numbers

Of course, proofreading numbers is much simpler when you understand the general rules for number usage in business correspondence. Follow these rules when using numbers:

1. In general, spell out numbers from 1 through 10, and use figures for numbers above 10. However, be consistent in using numbers within a sentence. Also, spell out a number that begins a sentence. Reword if it is awkward to spell out a number.

   Only *seven* people are on the panel.
   Two supervisors, *six* managers, and *thirteen* assistants were at the seminar. (All numbers are spelled out for consistency.)

2. Use figures for amounts of money, technical measurements and specifications, percentages, and fractions (unless the numeral would begin the sentence). Also use numerals to express time with the expression *o'clock* and with *a.m.* or *p.m.*

$25,475	$1324.56	79 cents
7.5 percent	2.4 feet	a 6:1 ratio
2 o'clock	7:15 a.m.	11 1/4

Omit *.00* in whole dollar amounts, and omit *:00* for time "on the hour." Use the word *cents* for amounts under a dollar; use the symbol ¢ in statistical writing or in columns when space is restricted. Spell out the word *percent*; use the symbol % in statistical writing or in columns when space is restricted. To construct fractions, use the diagonal key (/) (12 7/6 by 24 9/16 inches). Note that no comma is needed in four-digit numbers to separate thousands from hundreds: 3500.

3. Spell out ages (except in technical writing), indefinite numbers and amounts, and fractions that stand alone.

He will probably retire at age *sixty-two.*
We spent *hundreds* of dollars.
We need a *two-thirds* majority.

4. Use numerals in dates as follows:

We opened our store on September 6, 1986.
We opened our store on September 6.
But: We opened our store on the *6th* of September.

● **4-1** Circle the correct number style from the two choices given in parentheses in the following memorandum. (20 points each correct choice)

MEMORANDUM

To: Executive Committee   From: Alicia Walters

Subject: Office Renovation   Date: August 20, 1987

By September (15th, 15), we must complete our proposal for renovating the office. This project will cost (1000s, thousands) of dollars, but we feel the benefits will exceed the costs.

All (3, three) bids are (20, twenty) percent above our original estimates, and we have asked that the bids be resubmitted within (5, five) days. The companies have agreed to this time limit.

AW

pw

● **4-2** Circle the correct number style from the two choices given in parentheses in the following memorandum. (20 points each correct choice)

MEMORANDUM

To: Tom Simon   From: Sheila Oxford

Subject: Successful Sales Promotion   Date: September 1, 1987

Congratulations, Tom! You did a great job in selling the surplus television sets. (Two hundred, 200) advertising fliers were delivered to us by (9:00, 9) Monday morning. By Tuesday noon, they had been distributed to area homes.

Within (two, 2) days, we had sold all (twenty-five, 25) televisions at $499.95. This gave us a profit of ($100.00, $100) per set.

Thanks for your special efforts on this project.

SO

ws

● **4-3** Circle the correct number style from the two choices given in parentheses. (20 points each correct choice)

MEMORANDUM

To: Staff Members   From: Phil Canfield

Subject: Camp Filled to Capacity   Date: June 26, 1987

On June (25, 25th), our summer program began for teenage campers up to age (fifteen, 15). The bunk houses are filled to our capacity of (two hundred and twenty-five, 225).

For the first time in (five, 5) years, we have more boys than girls. In fact, almost (2/3, two-thirds) of our campers are boys. Your recruiting efforts have been successful. Keep up the good work!

PC

ldp

● **4-4** Circle the correct number style from the two choices given in parentheses in the following memorandum. (20 points each correct choice)

MEMORANDUM

Date: August 1, 1987

To: Concession Workers

From: Alex Brentworth, Personnel Manager

Subject: Concessions at Industrial League Games

Last night, the concession stand sales were $1922.85. We sold (twelve, 12) cases of soft drinks, six boxes of candy, and three dozen helium-filled balloons.

Our profit is (25%, 25 percent) of the total sales figure. To increase this percentage, we plan to raise the price of soft drinks to ($.50, 50 cents) each. This new price will be effective with our next game, which is scheduled for the (fifth, 5th) of August.

Concession operations have had a profit of ($21,000.00, $21,000) this summer. This money has been contributed to the charities you specified.

Thanks for your hard work.

                              AB

cew

Proofreading Review

● **4-A** Companies often send press releases to newspapers, magazines, and television and radio stations to publicize information. Proofread the following press release, correcting all number usage errors.

PRESS RELEASE

July 15, 19--

<u>To Be Released 10 A.M., July 15: Jacksonville, Florida--</u>

David P. Yezek, president of Fast Food Industries, Inc., announced plans to build executive offices and a warehouse distribution center 5 miles south of Jacksonville. The office complex will have twenty-five private offices and 12 executive office suites. The warehouse will have seven hundred thousand square feet of storage space.

Mr. Yezek said that his company completed the purchase of fifty acres of land yesterday and that construction will begin immediately. Fast Food will employ seventy-five people when the firm opens on December 6th. However, employment will grow to about 200 within the 1st year of operation. This new facility represents an investment of well over $3,000,000.

Fast Food Industries, Inc., has 2 small warehouse locations in each state. It provides food and utensil items to restaurants throughout the United States.

● **4-B** One of your employees, Hal Berkwith, received a $300 cash advance for a business trip to San Francisco. When he returned, he gave his secretary his pocket calendar, in which he had listed his expenses. As supervisor, it is your responsibility to proofread all expense reports. Correct any errors you find in the expense report on page 52 by striking through the error and writing the correction beside it. If you find no errors, sign the report in the blank that follows *Approved by.* Then complete the following questions:

1. Is the daily total correct for Monday? _____   If not, give the correct amount. _____

2. Is the daily total correct for Tuesday? _____   If not, give the correct amount. _____

3. Is the daily total correct for Wednesday? _____   If not, give the correct amount. _____

4. Is the daily total correct for Thursday? _____   If not, give the correct amount. _____

5. Is the weekly total correct? _____   If not, give the correct amount. _____

6. Are the dates correct? _____   If not, which one is incorrect? _____

7. Is the amount of the advance correct? _____   If not, give the correct amount. _____

8. Is the total due to the employee correct? _____   If not, give the correct amount. _____

9. Is the total due to the company correct? _____   If not, give the correct amount. _____

10. As supervisor, would you sign the blank marked *Approved by* indicating that the form is correct?

_____ If not, why not? _____

_____

Monday, August 10, 19--

Home to Atlanta Airport
    25 miles at 20¢/mile
Atlanta to San Francisco and return
    plane ticket $479
Taxi $12
Dinner $18.50
Hotel $70/night

Tuesday, August 11, 19--

Breakfast $5
Lunch $6.20
Dinner $14.85
Taxi $8.50
Hotel $70/night

Wednesday, August 12, 19--

Breakfast $5
Lunch $4.25
Dinner $15.25 (for me)
Dinner $18.95 (for client)
Entertainment
    Two concert tickets $35 (Total)
Taxi $9.50
Hotel $70/night

Thursday, August 13, 19--

Breakfast $5
Taxi $1.50
Car storage at airport $12
Atlanta airport to home
    25 miles at 20¢/mile

EXPENSE REPORT for: Hal Berkwith

Week Ending: 8/14/--

Date	Public Conveyance Kind	Public Conveyance Amount	Personal Automobile Mileage	Personal Automobile Amount	Hotel Amount	Meals Amount	Other Expenses Itemize	Other Expenses Amount	Daily Total
8/10	Plane	$479.00	25 @ 20¢	$5.00	$70.00	$18.50			$584.50
	Taxi	$12.00							
8/11	Taxi	$8.50			$70.00	$5.00			$104.55
						$6.20			
						$14.85			
8/12	Taxi	$9.50			$70.00	$5.00	Concert tickets	$35.00	$154.25
						$4.25	Client's dinner	$15.25	
						$15.25			
8/13	Taxi	$7.50	25 @ 20¢	$5.00		$5.00	Car storage	$12.00	$29.50

Weekly Total:	$872.80
Advance, If Any:	$300.00
Total Due Employee:	$572.80
Total Due Company:	00

Purpose of Travel: Contacting prospective clients

Submitted by: Hal Berkwith   Date: 8/15/--

Approved by: Date:

Billing Code: Selling Expense

5.

Styles and Formats for Letters and Memos

Letters

There are several letter styles appropriate for office use. The ones most widely used are illustrated in this chapter. These are as follows: the block style; the modified-block style, standard format; the modified-block style with indented paragraphs; and the simplified style. The stick examples below will help you become familiar with the letter styles quickly and easily. Letter parts are identified as follows:

D	Date line	M	Message	RI	Reference initials
I	Inside address	C	Complimentary closing	SB	Subject line
Sl	Salutation	W	Writer's identification		

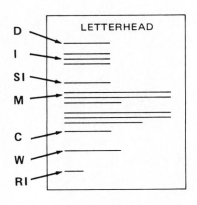

Block Style. The block style is the most consistent style. Each line begins at the left margin; there are no paragraph indentions.

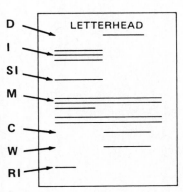

Modified-Block Style—Standard Format. In this format, the date line, complimentary closing, and writer's identification all begin at the center.

53

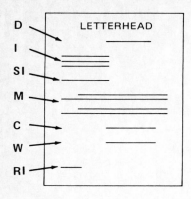

Modified-Block Style—With Indented Paragraphs. This letter style is like the standard modified-block style except that the paragraphs are indented five spaces.

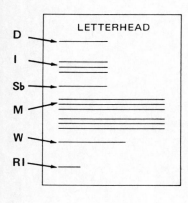

Simplified Style. This modern style omits the salutation (S1) and the complimentary closing (C). A subject line, keyed in all-capital letters, is added. The writer's identification is also keyed in all-capital letters.

Frequently, businesses adopt one style for all letters. Some businesses let each writer choose the style. Styles should never be mixed within the same letter.

Another element of letter style is punctuation. There are two basic punctuation styles: standard and open. Only two lines of the letter are affected—the salutation and the complimentary closing.

In standard punctuation style, a colon is used after the salutation and a comma after the complimentary closing. Most writers prefer this style, which is shown in the letters on page 55.

In open punctuation style, the colon after the salutation and the comma after the complimentary closing are omitted, as shown in the modified-block style letter on page 56.

Several special notations are needed to make some letters complete. Examples of these are the enclosure and mailing notations, attention line, subject line, and courtesy copy (cc) notations (see the letters on pages 55–56). The term *courtesy copy* replaces the term *carbon copy,* because the majority of copies are no longer carbon copies. They are photostatic or electronically produced copies.

▼▼ Proofreading Pointers

▼ When proofreading a letter, make sure that it follows one format style and one punctuation style consistently.

▼ Always be sure to check that the date, reference initials, and other parts of a letter have not been omitted.

582 South Blauvelt Avenue
Sioux Falls, South Dakota 57103
March 27, 1987 ↓2

Reference: File 3428 ↓3

Better Business Bureau
Post Office Box 2849
Sioux Falls, South Dakota 57103 ↓2

Attention: Consumer Products Division ↓2

Ladies and Gentlemen: ↓2

On March 5, I wrote you concerning a product purchased from ABC Toys, Inc. I was convinced that the toy was unsafe for the ages recommended on the package label. ↓2

ABC Toys, Inc., contacted the manufacturer and found that there was a misprint on the label. The label will be corrected on the next printing. ↓2

Thank you for your help in getting this correction made. ↓2

Very truly yours, ↓4

(Mrs.) Elizabeth D. Starr

Elizabeth D. Starr

MODIFIED-BLOCK STYLE—STANDARD FORMAT
STANDARD PUNCTUATION

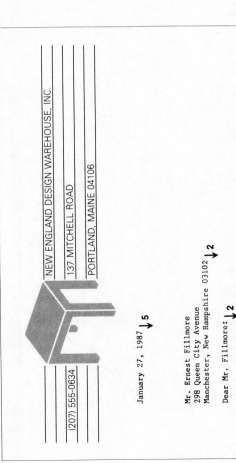

NEW ENGLAND DESIGN WAREHOUSE, INC.
137 MITCHELL ROAD
PORTLAND, MAINE 04106
(207) 555-0634

January 27, 1987 ↓5

Mr. Ernest Fillmore
298 Queen City Avenue
Manchester, New Hampshire 03102 ↓2

Dear Mr. Fillmore: ↓2

Subject: Your Order 2458 ↓2

Thank you for your order 2458 dated January 20, 1987. We have all the items you ordered except the lamp, catalog 431-L. We expect to be able to ship the lamp February 15. ↓2

Do you want us to hold your entire order until February 15, or do you want partial shipment? Please let us know your wishes so that we can serve you better. ↓2

Sincerely yours, ↓2

NEW ENGLAND DESIGNS, INC. ↓4

Otto Preston

Otto Preston ↓2

jmb
cc Ms. Denise Branscomb

BLOCK STYLE
STANDARD PUNCTUATION

Quality Printing Company
2116 Grant Street
Pittsburgh, Pennsylvania 15219
(412) 555-3425

June 27, 1987 ↓2

CONFIDENTIAL ↓3

Ms. Andrea Mostern
Mostern Printing Company
3828 Adair Road
Chester, PA 19015 ↓2 ↓2

Dear Ms. Mostern ↓2

Since our meeting last week, I have been seriously considering your proposal to acquire our printing facility. The terms you offered are quite satisfactory. ↓2

However, your proposal calls for my employment services for five years. I prefer to retire and would appreciate your removing this obligation from the contract. ↓2

At our meeting, you requested copies of current financial statements. These are enclosed. ↓2

Sincerely yours ↓2

QUALITY PRINTING COMPANY ↓4

M. Todd Wilkins

M. Todd Wilkins
President ↓2

dt
Enclosure

MODIFIED-BLOCK STYLE—WITH INDENTED PARAGRAPHS
OPEN PUNCTUATION

FROZEN FOODS, INC.
225 West Woodlawn Road
Charlotte, North Carolina 28210
(704) 555-8648
FINE FOODS SINCE 1925

October 30, 1987 ↓5

Mr. Alex Oberlin
Mechanical Repairs, Inc.
1825 Birchdale Drive
Winston Salem, NC 27106 ↓3

MAINTENANCE CONTRACT #65232-L ↓3

Alex, please renew our maintenance contract effective November 15. We understand that there will be a 10 percent increase due to the age of our equipment. ↓2

Your service representative has arranged a preventative maintenance inspection on November 30. At that time, the representative will give us recommendations on replacing outdated equipment. ↓2

We appreciate your prompt service and your expert advice. Both of these help us keep our customers satisfied. ↓5

Samuel Bronson

SAMUEL BRONSON—PRESIDENT ↓2

kst

SIMPLIFIED STYLE

● **5-1** The following are all correct. Name the letter style in the space provided below. (25 points each correct identification)

1.

LETTERHEAD

2.

LETTERHEAD

3.

LETTERHEAD

4.

LETTERHEAD

1. _____

2. _____

3. _____

4. _____

● **5-2** Some of the following stick examples are correct; some are not. Examine each carefully. Then identify each correct letter style by writing its name in the space provided below the examples. If the example mixes different letter styles or omits a necessary part, write *x* in the space provided. (10 points each correct answer)

1.
LETTERHEAD

2.
LETTERHEAD

3.
LETTERHEAD

4.
LETTERHEAD

5.
LETTERHEAD

6.
LETTERHEAD

7.

LETTERHEAD

8.

LETTERHEAD

9.

LETTERHEAD

10.

LETTERHEAD

1. _____
2. _____
3. _____
4. _____
5. _____
6. _____
7. _____
8. _____
9. _____
10. _____

● **5-3** Before completing this exercise, examine the letters on pages 55–56 carefully, paying special attention to the spacing between parts of the letter. Then for the letter below, indicate in the spaces provided how many times you should operate the return lever or return key at each location. (10 points each correct answer)

February 21, 1987

1. _____

Mr. Philip Lopez
8219 Della Road, S.W.
Albuquerque, NM 87105

2. _____

Dear Mr. Lopez:

3. _____

Subject: Accounting Position

4. _____

Yesterday we received your resume and letter requesting
an employment interview. Your background is impressive, and
we would like to talk with you concerning your career plans.

5. _____

We plan to increase our accounting staff in June. Since this
is about the time you will be graduated from college, it
may be that you would like to begin your professional career
with Carter Construction Company.

6. _____

Please come for an interview on Friday, March 10, at 3 p.m.
If this time is not convenient for you, call me to arrange
another time.

Sincerely yours,

7. _____

CARTER CONSTRUCTION COMPANY

8. _____

R. William Carter
Vice President

9. _____
10. _____

sh

Score: _____

Memorandums

Another message format commonly used for business communications is the memorandum. The letter is used to write to people *outside* the company, and the memorandum is used to write to employees *within* the company.

A letter is more formal than a memorandum. Letters generally include salutations and complimentary closings, and they always try to build goodwill. Memorandums are designed to be efficient and time-saving.

Many companies use memorandum forms on which the guide words *Date, To, From,* and *Subject* are printed. This saves time; when printed forms are not used, the operator must key in the guide words on plain paper. Depending on length, memos may be on a full page (8½ by 11 inches) or a half page (8½ by 5½ inches).

Study the following examples of memo forms. As you do, you will notice that the guide words can be arranged in different patterns. You will also notice that when keyboarded on plain paper, the guide words can be in all-capital letters or in initial capitals only. The trend is to use initial capitals only because this seems to be easier when using automated equipment.

---

interoffice memorandum

To   All Employees   From   Alice Macmillan

Subject   Spring Courses   Date   December 7, 1987 ↓ 3

The Office Training Center is pleased to announce the courses available next spring through our Continuing Education Program. As you will see from the enclosed brochure, many on-the-job skill refresher courses will again be offered: Gregg shorthand, typewriting, word processing, business math, and so on. In addition to professional development courses, personal development courses are again included: language arts courses, music and crafts, as well as language courses (conversational German, Italian, French, and Spanish). ↓ 2

In response to the requests of many employees for writing-improvement courses, we have included three new programs for spring--programs especially designed for the business writer: ↓ 2

    Writing Persuasive Communications

        Mr. James K. Broome, Allen Business College
        Thursday, 3:30-5:30, Room 201

    Legal Aspects of Business Writing

        Ms. Barbara Schlain, Associate Counsel, Legal Department
        Wednesday, 3:30-5:30, Room 206

    Developing Proofreading Skill

        Ms. Nancy Glenn, Office Training Center Staff
        Tuesday, 3:30-5:30, Room 204

Complete details, as well as registration forms, are provided in the brochure. Space will be limited, so please register no later than February 8! ↓ 2

                                        AM ↓ 2

gb
Enclosure

MEMORANDUM ON PRINTED FORM

(One-Inch Top Margin)

↓7

MEMORANDUM ↓3

DATE   October 29, 1987 ↓2

TO   Fred Nosker, Office Manager ↓2

FROM   Linda Vanderford, President ↓2

SUBJECT   New Office Hours ↓3

Beginning immediately, our office will open at 8:30 a.m. and close
at 5:30 p.m. We will continue to have the staggered lunch breaks from
11:30 a.m. to 1:30 p.m. ↓2

This change has been requested by both employees and customers.
Few customers call before 8:30 a.m., but many try to call
after 5 p.m. ↓2

Please let me know how this new schedule works. ↓2

LV ↓2

bh

MEMORANDUM ON PLAIN PAPER—GUIDE WORDS IN ALL CAPITALS

(One-Inch Top Margin)

↓7

MEMORANDUM ↓3

Date: November 9, 1987 ↓2

To: Linda Vanderford, President ↓2

From: Fred Nosker, Office Manager ↓2

Subject: New Office Hours ↓3

In reply to your memo of October 29 about changing our office
hours to 8:30 a.m. until 5:30 p.m., everything is working well. ↓2

This change was well received by the employees and by our customers.
Last week, we logged 145 calls after 5 p.m. This may increase when all
of our customers learn about our new hours. ↓2

FN ↓2

je

MEMORANDUM ON PLAIN PAPER—GUIDE WORDS IN INITIAL CAPITALS

● **5-4** Read the following memo, and then answer the ten questions below.
(10 points each correct answer)

MEMORANDUM

TO   Inez P. Johnson, Personnel Manager

  FROM   Amelia Langdon, President

SUBJECT   Needed Personnel

My secretary, Christa Canton, resigned yesterday because of her
health. She is planning to work until the end of the month.

    Please initiate your usual procedures to fill this vacancy.
I would like to hire someone as soon as possible so that before
Christa leaves she can help train the new secretary.

Friday afternoon would be a good time to interview applicants.

                        AL

---

1. What part of the heading is omitted? _____

2. List the four lines as they would appear on a printed form.

   _____   _____

   _____   _____

3. Should the lines in the heading be single-spaced or double-spaced? _____

4. Should the lines in the heading be in all-capital letters? _____

5. Other than the omitted part of the heading, what is wrong with the way the heading is typed?

   _____

6. After the heading, the return should be pressed _____ times before beginning the body.

7. The body of the above memorandum was single-spaced. Is single spacing correct? _____

8. There is an obvious error in the body of the memorandum. What is it? _____

   _____

9. What do the initials *AL* stand for? _____

10. There is a double space between the paragraphs in the above memorandum. Is this spacing correct?

   _____

● **5-5** For the memo on the next page, indicate in the space provided how
many times you should operate the return lever or return key at each location.
(10 points each correct answer)

(From top of page)   1. ____

MEMORANDUM   2. ____

DATE   March 5, 1987   3. ____

TO   Sheila Anderson, President   4. ____

FROM   Alan Warez, Plant Safety Superintendent   5. ____

SUBJECT   Fire Inspection   6. ____

On Wednesday, March 13, the local fire department   7. ____
will inspect our plant for possible fire hazards. They
will begin the inspection at noon.   8. ____

Do you think I should send a memorandum announcing
the inspection to each department head, or should the
inspection team find us just as we are with no
preparation?   9. ____

                    AW   10. ____

jb

Proofreading Review

● **5-A** In the space provided, answer the following questions on letter and
memorandum style.

List the four letter styles studied in this chapter.

1. _____

2. _____

3. _____

4. _____

List the two punctuation styles used in letters.

5. _____

6. _____

Which letter style omits the salutation and the complimentary closing?

7. _____

Which letter style uses all-capital letters for the subject line and the writer's identification?

8. _____

List the four main guide words in a memorandum.

9. _____

10. _____

11. _____

12. _____

Circle *T* if a statement is true. Circle *F* if it is false.

13. It is acceptable to mix letter styles within a letter if it looks nice. 13. T F

14. The guide words in a memorandum can be typed with initial capitals only or in all capitals. 14. T F

15. One punctuation style for letters uses a semicolon after the salutation and a comma after the complimentary closing. 15. T F

16. Memorandums may be typed on a full sheet or a half sheet. 16. T F

17. Paragraphs in the body of a memorandum and the message of a letter are single-spaced. 17. T F

18. It is standard procedure to double-space between paragraphs. 18. T F

19. Some companies use memorandum forms with the guide words printed on them. 19. T F

20. Letters are used to write people inside the company; memorandums are used to write people outside the company. 20. T F

● **5-B** Proofread the following letter. Use proofreaders' marks to indicate necessary corrections.

School of Nursing
COUNTY COMMUNITY COLLEGE
Post Office Box 48294   Spokane, Washington 99207   (509) 555-9954

April 2, 19--

Mrs. Margaret M. McKenna, President
Medical Testing Equipment and Supplies
Post Office Box 69424
Spokane, WA 99207-9424

Dear Mrs. McKenna;

Our student nursing association is planning a health fair to be
be held in our student center from 8:30 a.m. to 4:30 p.m. on May 1 and
May 2. The fair will be open tothe academic community and to area residents.

This is a community service project our for organization adn will
involve free screening for blood pressure, hearing, visual, and dental
problems. Dentists, nurses, physicians, and their assistants are giving
the tests and presenting seminars no health isssues.

Our organization also wants to provide information on home testing
products. Because you are a supplier of medical testing equipment and
supplies,you are invited to have a booth during the fair.

Please let me by April 15 if you can accept our invitation. Your
participation is essential in making our project a complete success.

Sincerely,

Robert Helton

ld

6.

Capitalization Alertness

Applying the Rules

You have probably already noticed that capital letters play a very special role in business writing. You learned, for example, that capital letters have particular uses in letter and memorandum formats. Review those formats and study the following capitalization rules carefully; they frequently cause problems in business writing.

1. Capitalize the first word in each sentence.

   Your copy of the report is enclosed.

2. Capitalize the names of particular people, places, and things.

   Mrs. Blanche Norris

   Pyrex plates

   Denver, Colorado

3. Capitalize titles when they are part of a person's name. Do not capitalize titles when they follow or further explain a person's name, except in an inside address.

   Anthony Luciano, visiting professor, phoned Professor Timothy O'Brien.

   Anthony Luciano, Visiting Professor
   Department of Economics
   University of Bridgeport
   Bridgeport, CT 06602

4. Do *not* capitalize common nouns.

   man

   woman

   plates

   city

   state

67

5. Capitalize the first word in the salutation of a letter. Within the salutation, also capitalize all nouns and titles.

   Dear Mr. Houser,

   Ladies and Gentlemen:

   Dear Ms. Baxter and Professor Harris

6. Capitalize only the first word in the complimentary closing of a letter.

   Sincerely yours,

   Very truly yours,

   Cordially yours,

7. Capitalize the days of the week, months of the year, and holidays. Seasons of the year are *not* capitalized.

Sunday, Monday	winter	Easter
Fourth of July	June, July	

8. Do *not* capitalize *a.m.* or *p.m.*

   10 a.m.   12 p.m.

9. When using the simplified letter style, type the subject line and the writer's identification in capital letters.

10. Use all capitals for coined acronyms and certain abbreviations. (When in doubt, check a dictionary.)

    She studied BASIC, FORTRAN, and COBOL.

    Adam is a CPA.

11. Use *either* all capitals *or* underscores with initial capitals for book titles, but be consistent within a communication.

    I read COMPUTERS IN EDUCATION.

    or

    I read Computers in Education.

12. In article titles, use initial capitals for the first word and all other words that are not articles or short prepositions. (Article titles are enclosed in quotation marks.)

    The title of his article was "Word Processing for Executives."

13. Use capitals appropriately in memorandum guide words. Use either all capitals or initial capitals only.

DATE:	Date:
TO:	To:
FROM:	From:
SUBJECT:	Subject:

14. Use all capitals for two-letter state abbreviations used in addresses.

Dr. Brandon DeCamp
St. Mary's Hospital
223 Third Street
Chicago, IL 60612

● **6-1** Capitals are used correctly in the following letter. To make sure you know why each underlined letter is correctly capitalized or *not* capitalized, write the number (1 to 14) of the rule above that applies. (10 points each rule identified correctly)

	Rule Number
<u>J</u>uly 3, 1987	1. _____
Mr. William Ragsdale, <u>CPA</u>	2. _____
356 Poly Drive	
Billings, <u>MT</u> 59101	3. _____
Dear Mr. <u>R</u>agsdale:	4. _____
Thank you for your telephone order for our computer	
software. As you requested, the order is being shipped	
by Express Mail with delivery guaranteed by 4 <u>p.m.</u>,	5. _____
<u>W</u>ednesday, July 5. The postal services will be	6. _____
closed for the <u>F</u>ourth of July holiday.	7. _____
<u>E</u>nclosed with this software is a complimentary copy of	8. _____
our latest book, <u>S</u>oftware for <u>A</u>ccountants. You will	9. _____
find it helpful in selecting additional software.	
<u>S</u>incerely yours,	10. _____

● **6-2**   In the following letter, which of the two items in parentheses is correct? Write the correct item in the space provided below. (10 points each correct answer)

1.   (June/june) 30, 1987

Mr. Peter Mandrell
550 Juntura Way
2.   Salem, (OR/Or) 97302

Dear Mr. Mandrell

3.   Congratulations! (Your/your) credit application has been gladly approved.

4.   Your (References/references), Mr. Mandrell, have a high opinion
5.   of you and your ability to meet your (Financial/financial) obligations. All of the responses to our inquiries were
6.   (Positive/positive).

7.   You may begin using your (Benson's/benson's) charge account today. You will receive a 10 percent discount on any purchases made during
8.   (July/july). This discount is in addition to our already low prices
9.   during our (Summer/summer) sale.

10.   Sincerely (Yours/yours)

Ralph A. Benson
Credit Manager

pc

1. _____   6. _____

2. _____   7. _____

3. _____   8. _____

4. _____   9. _____

5. _____   10. _____

● **6-3**   Use appropriate proofreaders' marks to indicate capitalization errors in the following items. (10 points each item)

1.   MEMORANDUM

   DATE
   TO
   FROM
   Subject
2. Alicia is a Certified Professional Secretary (cps).
3. The meeting begins at 10:30 A.M.
4. Wilbur's article, "Office lighting," was published last month.
5. Do you think that carmen ruiz should get the promotion?
6. Please order three copies of the book MEETING CORPORATE Goals.
7. Ask Max Fielding, our Company Accountant, for his opinion.
8. We will be closed from Christmas to new year's day.
9. They are going to a sales convention in chicago.
10. We hired professor Daryl Montief to be our consultant.

Proofreading Review

● **6-A** Use proofreaders' marks to correct the capitalization errors in the memorandum that follows.

MEMORANDUM

Date: June 1, 19--

To: Accounting Department

From: Sylvia Styler, Manager

SUBJECT: Annual Reports

Our Fiscal year ends June 30, and our company accountants will be here july 1-5 to help us prepare our annual reports. Harriet rentzel, cpa, will be here to oversee the process.

Harriet has asked to meet with us on monday, july 1, at 8:30 A.M. This is an organizational meeting which she feels will get us off to a good start.

Even though it is a Paid holiday, we do plan for the accounting staff to work on the fourth of July. staff members may take two days off during July or August to compensate them for working on a Holiday.

                              SS

mkp

● **6-B** The letter below was completed in the word processing center of your firm. Changes were needed after it was transcribed. Mark the following changes using proofreaders' marks. (Of course, the letter will have to be printed again, but it will not have to be rekeyboarded, because it was stored in the word processing system.)

Changes

1. The shipment will be made Friday instead of Wednesday.
2. Shipment will be made by common carrier.
3. There are only 800 yards instead of 850 yards of Style 2246.
4. There are 350 yards instead of 250 yards of Style 1431.
5. Credit has been approved for $10,000 instead of $5,500.
6. Andrew Ross transferred to another branch. Questions should be directed to Linda Wong.
7. The new sample sheets are not back from the printer. They will be mailed next week.
8. Barbara Straub was promoted to sales manager.

QUALITY FABRICS, INC.

Post Office Box 1425
Wichita, Kansas 67208
(316) 555-4051

December 4, 19--

Ms. Miriam Samuels
The Suit Factory
4187 East Vesta Drive
Wichita, KS 67208

Dear Ms. Samuels:

    Your Order 1842 will be shipped on Wednesday, December 9, by our truck. The following quantities will be shipped to you:

Style 2246	Executive Stripe	850 yards
Style 6615	Traditional Navy	600 yards
Style 1431	Business Gray	250 yards

    We are pleased to give you credit up to $5500. Should you have questions concerning this, please call Andrew Ross. Your business is appreciated.

    Our new sample sheets are enclosed. These are the new summer colors.

Sincerely yours,

Barbara Straub
Assistant Sales Manager

Comma Usage

Applying the Rules

The comma and the period are the two most frequently used punctuation marks, and the comma is the most frequently misused. To make sure that you understand when to use a comma—and when not to use a comma—study the following few rules. These are the rules that will apply most often in business writing.

The comma is used in certain letter parts:

1. In the *date line*, the day and the year are separated by a comma.

   January 12, 1982

   Within a sentence, use two commas to set off the year when it follows the month and day.

   On May 1, 1988, we plan to move.

   The budgets are due on December 1, 1989, so that the 1990 forecasts can be made.

2. In *inside addresses* and *return addresses*, the city and state names are always separated by a comma.

   Fargo, North Dakota 58102
   Joplin, MO 64801

   Within a sentence, use two commas to set off the name of a state when it follows the name of a city.

   He moved to Joplin, *Missouri*, in 1979.

   McNulty Company headquarters is being moved to Houston, Texas, early next year.

Also, use a comma after each part of an address.

Please write to Mr. John Neel, 532 East Tanner Street, Knoxville, Tennessee 37916, if you need additional information.

3. In the *writer's identification line,* a comma is used to separate the writer's name and title if both are on the same line.

Harriet A. Trask, Treasurer

However, no comma separates the two when they are on two lines.

Harriet A. Trask
Treasurer

4. In the *complimentary closing,* a comma is used at the end of the line (in standard punctuation style).

Sincerely yours,
Cordially,

Look again at the letters on pages 55–56 to see how commas appear in these letter parts.

Commas are also used in the bodies of letters, memos, and reports—in all writing.

5. Commas are used to set off names used in direct address.

Do you agree, *John,* that we should approve this expense? (John is the person spoken to, the name in direct address.)

6. Commas are used to separate three or more items in a series.

Kent, Lara, and Carole were asked to revise their estimates.

We called Mrs. Ibsen, discussed the problem, and asked for her advice.

7. Commas are used to set off words or phrases in apposition.

Mr. DePalma, *our general manager,* is on vacation.

Mrs. Xavier, *owner of the property,* has hired a real estate agent.

The phrases in italics are called *appositives. Our general manager* is another way of saying *Mr. DePalma. Owner of the property* is another way of saying *Mrs. Xavier.* Appositives are always set off with two commas (unless, of course, they appear at the end of a sentence).

8. Commas are used before the conjunction in a compound sentence.

Anthony wanted to attend the convention, *but* his manager limited the number of people who could go.

Bertha did most of the research for the report, *and* she also wrote the first draft.

9. Commas are used after introductory words, phrases, and clauses.

Yes, the new price is $9.95.

Incidentally, Mrs. Warren was promoted to regional manager last month.

To be eligible for the rebate, customers must show proof of purchase.

When Ms. Silver arrives, please give her this package.

10. Commas are used to separate two or more adjectives that modify the same noun.

They developed a *bright, interesting* brochure to send to all customers.

Mr. Jonas always writes *long, rambling, wordy* reports.

11. Commas are used to separate parenthetical comments from the rest of the sentence.

In my opinion, we should conduct a marketing survey.

We should, *in my opinion,* conduct a marketing survey.

Review these comma rules carefully; make sure you understand them before you continue.

▼▼ Proofreading Pointers

▼ Proofread carefully for comma errors because the comma is the most frequently misused punctuation mark.

▼ When in doubt about comma usage, check a reference or style manual.

● **7-1** The commas in the following letter are used correctly. Referring to the rule numbers at the beginning of this chapter, place the appropriate rule number (1 to 11) for the use of each underlined comma in the space provided in the right margin. (10 points each correct rule number)

Rule
Number

May 30, 1987

1. _____

Ms. Jacquelyn Ward
3400 Cooper Road
Little Rock, AR 72204

2. _____

Dear Ms. Ward:

Thank you for your interest in the Sea Breeze Hotel. When you visit us, you will enjoy an ocean-front suite designed for comfort and relaxation.

3. _____

Randy Holman, our entertainment coordinator, will help you

4. _____

arrange activities for your family. Free golf, tennis, and

5. _____

scuba diving will be part of your vacation package. You may choose to take advantage of our modern, well-equipped health

6. _____

spa. You may decide, however, to enjoy a relaxing walk on the beach.

7. _____

You are sure to find vacation fun, Ms. Ward, when you visit

8. _____

us in Myrtle Beach, South Carolina.

Sincerely yours,

9. _____

Alex Lopez, Manager

10. _____

1t

● **7-2** In the following memorandum, the keyboard operator got "comma happy" and added ten unnecessary commas. Use the delete symbol (ϒ) to strike through these unneeded commas.

MEMORANDUM

Date: August 15, 1987

To: Al Symbosky, General Manager

From: Julia Cantrell, Personnel Manager

Subject: Office Salaries

As you requested in your March 15, memorandum, I have completed an analysis of our office salaries. The compensation package offered to our staff, compares favorably with that of similar companies, in our area.

Salary increments, are based on job performance, responsibility incurred, and necessary qualifications as specified in the job description. Annual evaluations, of these factors, determine the amount of merit increase, given to each employee.

In a recent employee survey, 95 percent of our employees approved of this method of review. About 90 percent, felt that their salary and benefit package was the best one offered in our county. This satisfaction is substantiated by a low, turnover rate.

I recommend no changes in our salary package, but will monitor the situation closely for the next three months.

JC

kpf

Proofreading Review

● **7-A** Most of the commas are omitted in the following two letters. Use proofreaders' marks to add commas where needed.

BAXTER
Manufacturing Co., Inc.

Post Office Box 8944, Charlotte, North Carolina 28212
(704) 555-8824

December 9 1987

Mr. Steven Okamoto CPA
Ross, Ross, Redding, and Company
8614 Nathanel Lane
Charlotte NC 28212

Dear Mr. Okamoto:

We would like to arrange a time for your annual audit of our books. Ms. Carol Sifford our senior accountant would like you to come as early in January as possible. She thought this might be a convenient time to give you the information necessary for completing our corporate tax returns.

As we have done in previous years we will let you and your staff stay in the company guest house. Please let me know how many of your people will be with you.

I have several questions that are too involved for this brief letter and I would appreciate your calling me next week. The questions relate to the anticipated July 1, 1988 sale of our property in Atlanta.

Sincerely yours

BAXTER MANUFACTURING CO., INC.

George Trull Treasurer

ht

BAXTER
Manufacturing Co., Inc.
Post Office Box 8944, Charlotte, North Carolina 28212
(704) 555-8824

December 9, 1987

Rose B. Mowery Ph.D.
1212 South Tryon Street
Charlotte, NC 28212

Dear Dr. Mowery:

Your seminar on managerial communications was excellent! Our managers
attending your intensive session on Friday December 2 agree that you
provided them with many valuable tools for effective productive
communication with employees at all levels. They said that you are
interesting knowledgeable, and entertaining.

The president of our company Mr. Harry Dilworth plans to attend your
next seminar, which I know will be equally successful. He has read your
recent articles and wants to meet you personally.

Thank you again Dr. Mowery for conducting this beneficial seminar for
our managers. Incidentally I have cleared my calendar so that I can
attend your next one.

Sincerely,

BAXTER MANUFACTURING CO., INC.

Helen Reynolds, Director
Executive Development Committee

tw

● **7-B** Below is a handwritten draft of a program for a company-sponsored executive development workshop. At the bottom of the program is a coupon for employee registration. The draft was given to a word processing operator with instructions to put it in an attractive format. Compare the draft with the printed copy on the next page. Use proofreaders' marks to indicate any corrections on the printed copy. Put a small check to the left of each printed line that is correct.

Executive Development Workshop
LANDRUM COMPANY
Friday, October 1, 19--
and Saturday, October 2, 19--
Community Conference Center
912 Center Drive, Evansville, Indiana

Human Relations and Productivity

Friday

7:00 - 7:30
Registration and Snack
Second Floor Lounge

7:30 - 8:30
Ms. Martha Woolery
Conference Room 1102

8:30 - 10:00
Movie -- The Problem Employee
Audiovisual Room

Saturday

8:00 - 8:30
Coffee and Pastries
Second Floor Lounge

Saturday (Continued)

8:30 - 10:00
Dr. Steven Chapple
Conference Room 2108

10:00 - 10:30
Juice and Fruit Snack
First Floor Lounge

10:30 - 12:00
Role Playing Activities
Auditorium

12:00 - 1:30
Luncheon
Main Dining Room

1:30 - 3:00
Mrs. Olga Breitman
Conference Room 2122

3:00 - 4:00
Conclusion and Evaluation
Conference Room 1105

I plan to attend the workshop, Human Relations and Productivity.

Name:_____
Position:_____
Department:_____
Phone Extension:_____

Executive Development Workshop
LANDRUM COMPANY
Friday, October 1, 19--
and Saturday, October 2, 19--
Community Conference Center
912 Center Drive, Evansville, Indiana

Human Relations and Productivity

Friday

7:00-7:30	Registration and Snack	Second Floor Lounge
7:30-8:30	Ms. Martha Woolery	Conference Room 1102
8:30-10:00	Movie--The Problem Employee	Audiovisual Room

Saturday

8:00-8:30	Coffee and Pastries	Second Floor Lounge
8:30-10:00	Dr. Steven Chapple	Conference Room 2108
10:00-10:30	Juice and Fruit Snack	First Floor Lounge
10:30-12:00	Role Playing Activities	Auditorium
12:00-1:30	Luncheon	Main Dining Room
1:30-3:00	Mrs. Olga Breitman	Conference Room 2122
3:00-4:00	Conclusion and Evaluation	Conference Room 1105

I plan to attend the workshop, Human Relations and Productivity.

Name: _____

Position: _____

Departmnet: _____

Phone Extension: _____

Spelling and Word Division

Helpful Tools

Millions of dictionaries are sold each year, because everybody needs a dictionary. If you consider yourself a poor speller, don't worry. You can improve your spelling skills greatly by paying special attention to a few general rules and by getting into the habit of using a dictionary. Whenever you're not sure how to spell a word, look it up in a dictionary or a word reference book.

Your dictionary is a valuable tool. As you can see by the entry for *receive,* it tells you more than just how to spell the word.

It tells you how to divide the word at the end of a line (*re-ceive*). It tells you *receive* is a verb (*vb*), and it gives you the principal parts of that verb (*received* as in "I have received" and *receiving* as in "I am receiving"). It gives the different meanings of *receive* as well as examples of how the word is commonly used in phrases and sentences. As a further help, synonyms for *receive* are shown in all-capital letters (*acquire, admit, welcome*).

> **re·ceiv·ables** \-bəlz\ *n pl* (1917) : amounts of money receivable
> **re·ceive** \ri-'sēv\ *vb* **re·ceived; re·ceiv·ing** [ME *receiven,* fr. ONF *receivre,* fr. L *recipere,* fr. *re-* + *capere* to take — more at HEAVE] *vt* (14c) **1 :** to come into possession of : ACQUIRE ⟨~ a gift⟩ **2 a :** to act as a receptacle or container for ⟨the cistern ~s water from the roof⟩ **b :** to assimilate through the mind or senses ⟨~ new ideas⟩ **3 a :** to permit to enter : ADMIT **b :** WELCOME, GREET **c :** to react to in a specified manner **4 :** to accept as authoritative, true, or accurate : BELIEVE **5 a :** to support the weight or pressure of : BEAR **b :** to take (a mark or impression) from the weight of something ⟨some clay ~s clear impressions⟩ **c :** ACQUIRE, EXPERIENCE ⟨*received* his early schooling at home⟩ **d :** to suffer the hurt or injury of ⟨*received* a broken nose⟩ ~ *vi* **1 :** to be a recipient **2 :** to be at home to visitors ⟨~s on Tuesdays⟩ **3 :** to convert incoming radio waves into perceptible signals **4 :** to catch or gain possession of a kicked ball in football
> **Received Pronunciation** *n* (1932) : the pronunciation of Received Standard

By permission. From *Webster's Ninth New Collegiate Dictionary* © 1986 by Merriam-Webster, Inc., publisher of the Merriam-Webster® Dictionaries.

Wordbooks are also helpful spelling references. Although they do not list all the information given in a dictionary, they do provide the essential word information most business writers need, and they provide this information in a handy format. Here, for example, is a page from *20,000+ Words* by Charles E. Zoubek, Gregg A. Condon, and Louis A. Leslie (8th Edition, Gregg Division, McGraw-Hill Book Company, New York, 1986).

88

fore·fin·ger	for·est·er	form·er n.
fore·foot	for·est·ry	for·mer·ly (previously;
fore·front	fore·tell	cf. *formally*)
fore·go	fore·thought	for·mi·da·ble
fore·go·ing	for·ev·er	form·less
fore·gone	fore·warn	for·mu·la
fore·ground	fore·wom·an	for·mu·la·rize
fore·hand	fore·word (preface; cf.	for·mu·late
fore·hand·ed	*forward*)	for·mu·la·tion
fore·head	for·feit	for·sake
for·eign	for·fei·ture	for·sooth
for·eign·er	for·gave	for·swear
fore·judge	forg·er	for·syth·ia
fore·knowl·edge	forg·ery	fort (stronghold; cf.
fore·lock	for·get·ful	*forte*)
fore·man	for·get–me–not	forte (talent; cf. *fort*)
fore·mast	for·get·ta·ble	forth (forward; cf.
fore·most	for·get·ting	*fourth*)
fore·name	for·give·ness	forth·com·ing
fore·noon	for·giv·ing	forth·right
fo·ren·sic	for·go	forth·with
fore·or·dain	for·got	for·ti·eth
fore·part	for·lorn	for·ti·fi·ca·tion
fore·quar·ter	for·mal	for·ti·fi·er
fore·run	form·al·de·hyde	for·ti·fy
fore·run·ner	for·mal·i·ty	for·tis·si·mo
fore·see	for·mal·ize	for·ti·tude
fore·see·able	for·mal·ly	fort·night
fore·shad·ow	(ceremonially; cf.	FOR·TRAN
fore·short·en	*formerly*)	for·tress
fore·sight	for·mat	for·tu·itous
for·est	for·ma·tion	for·tu·ity
fore·stall	for·ma·tive	for·tu·nate
for·es·ta·tion	for·mer adj.	for·tune

This wordbook gives you the spelling and word division for each entry and, when appropriate, shows capital letters for trade names, proper names, names of cities and states, and so on.

For example, it tells the user that FORTRAN (a computer language) is spelled in all-capital letters. The comments after some entries help you to distinguish between *formally* and *formerly*, between *fort* and *forte*, and so on. Hyphens in compound words are shown by long dashes, and an extra space between words shows that an entry is spelled as two separate words.

A wordbook is helpful to the business writer who wants to check spelling, capitalization, or word division quickly. Be sure to keep a dictionary *and* a wordbook handy when you are proofreading, writing, or typing.

Spelling Rules

There are many variations in spelling patterns in our language—so many, in fact, that there are few rules that have no exceptions. The following rules, however, will help you to avoid many of the most common errors in spelling. Pay careful attention to them.

1. **Ei and ie.** Usually, *ie* is used when the sound is *e*, and *ei* is used when the sound is *a* or when the *ie* follows the letter *c*.

ie: piece   believe   niece
ei: weigh   neighbor   eight
         receive   receipt   ceiling

2. **Silent *e*.** A silent *e* is usually dropped when a suffix beginning with a vowel is added to the word (a suffix is a word ending).

use + able = usable
disclose + ure = disclosure
believe + ing = believing
continue + ance = continuance

Words ending in *ee* (*agree, see*) do not drop an *e* (*agreeable, seeing*).
     A silent *e* is usually retained when a suffix beginning with a consonant is added to the word (a consonant is any letter other than *a, e, i, o,* and *u*).

achieve + ment = achievement
meddle + some = meddlesome
late + ness = lateness
leisure + ly = leisurely

3. **Words ending in *ie* or *y*.** For words ending in *ie*, change the *ie* to *y* before adding *ing*.

lie—lying   tie—tying

For words ending in a consonant plus *y*, change the *y* to *i* before adding a suffix.

involuntary + ly = involuntarily
heavy + er = heavier

If the suffix itself begins with an *i*, do not double the *i*.

library + ian = librarian

For words ending in a vowel plus *y*, keep the *y* and add the suffix.

play + er = player   say + ing = saying

4. **Doubling the final consonant.** A final consonant is doubled when a vowel comes before the consonant and a vowel begins the suffix.

plan + ing = planning
cup + ed = cupped
slim + est = slimmest
fat + y = fatty

A final consonant is *not* doubled when the suffix also begins with a consonant.

cup + ful = cupful

Notice that the words, *plan, cup, slim,* and *fat* are one-syllable words. For words of more than one syllable, the final consonant is doubled before a suffix beginning with a vowel *if the last syllable is accented.*

refer + ed = referred   (accent on *fer*)
begin + ing = beginning   (accent on *gin*)

differ + ed = differed   (accent on *dif*)
travel + ing = traveling   (acccent on *trav*)

5. **Special problems**. Beware of words ending in *ant, ent, ance, ence, able, ible, ise,* and *ize*. These words are very troublesome; when you are not absolutely sure of the spelling, look them up.

ant   defendant, resistant
ent   dependent, persistent
able dependable, likable
ible forcible, flexible
ance assistance, relevance
ence intelligence, occurrence
ise   televise, advertise
ize   summarize, criticize

Only one commonly used word ends in *yze: analyze*.

Words that sound alike or are spelled similarly frequently cause problems (*affect-effect, accept-except,* and *there-their-they're*). Use a reference manual or dictionary to check these similar words.

● **8-1** The following memorandum has ten spelling errors. Circle each error, and write the correct word in the space provided below and on the next page. (5 points each error circled and 5 points each word correctly spelled)

MEMORANDUM

Date: April 30, 1987

To: Henry Kreider

From: Shirley Lafferty

Subject: Sales Commission

Begining June 1, we will have a new sales commission rate of 8 percent. As you know, we have been offerring 6 percent. This new rate has been made posible by improving our manufactureing productivity and reducing our administrative costs.

We beleive that the increased productivity and the cost reductions are a direct result of implementing an automated information system. This system makes needed information readyly availible for management decisions such as planing, ordering, and scheduling more efficient.

This improvement is a big achievment. Thank you for your assistence.

SL

1. _____   3. _____

2. _____   4. _____

5. _____   8. _____

6. _____   9. _____

7. _____   10. _____

Spelling Verification Software

Some word processing software proofreads for spelling errors. The software highlights, or in some other way makes the operator aware of, words that are not recognized. The operator must then decide if the word is correct or incorrect.

Spelling verification software, often called a "spelling checker," has a dictionary of words that it recognizes. Operators can add words that are peculiar to their organizations. Proper names and technical words, such as medical and chemical terms, can be added to the dictionary so that the software can recognize them and not highlight them as potential errors.

Software that verifies spelling can lead us to a false sense of security. Look at this example:

It has been too months sense hour last meetnig.

The only error the spelling verification software would find would be *meetnig*. Did you find three more errors? The sentence should read as follows:

It has been *two* months *since our* last *meeting*.

Spelling verification software does not identify *correctly spelled* but *incorrectly used* words. The next exercise will give you practice in finding this kind of error.

● **8-2** Proofread the memorandum below, and circle each incorrectly used word. In the spaces provided below and on the next page, the memorandum, correct each word circled. (5 points each word correctly circled and 5 points each word corrected)

MEMORANDUM

DATE   May 20, 1987

TO   Calvin Symbosky

FORM   Larry Turbin

SUBJECT Telemarketing Workshop

Thank you for arranging the telemarketing workshop for hour sells staff. Beginning next month, all sales representatives will spend won day each weak in the office phoning potential customers. I won't them to no how to use this time effectively.

Too Saturday sessions should provide the time needed four developing some knew sales techniques.

LT

1. _____   6. _____
2. _____   7. _____
3. _____   8. _____
4. _____   9. _____
5. _____   10. _____

▼▼ Proofreading Pointers

▼ Be sure to keep a dictionary, a reference manual, and a wordbook handy when proofreading, writing, or keyboarding.

▼ Because spelling verification software will overlook incorrectly used words (*sale* for *sell* and *two* for *too*), be alert to correct meaning when you proofread.

Plurals

Spelling errors often occur in forming the plurals of nouns. Make sure you understand each of the following five rules for forming plurals:

1. Most plurals are formed by adding *s* to the singular forms.

   report + s = reports
   office + s = offices

2. When the singular ends in *s, x, z, ch,* or *sh,* add *es.*

   boss + es = bosses
   box + es = boxes
   church + es = churches
   bush + es = bushes
   Schwartz + es = Schwartzes
   Adams + es = Adamses

3. When the singular word ends in a vowel plus *y,* add *s.*

   boy + s = boys
   bay + s = bays

4. When the singular word ends in a consonant plus *y,* change the *y* to *i* and add *es.*

   company + ies = companies
   ply + ies = plies

5. To form the plural of a hyphenated or spaced compound, make the main word plural.

   mother-in-law + s = mothers-in-law

   For some nouns, there are few useful rules for forming plurals. You should know the plurals of these commonly used nouns: *man—men, woman—women, child—children,* and *foot—feet.*

When you do not know how to form the plural, use a dictionary.

● **8-3** Proofread the following letter for errors in plurals. Circle each error, and write the correct word in the space provided below. (5 points each error correctly circled and 5 points each error corrected)

_____

Dear Ms. O'Leary:

Enclosed are copys of the remodeling planes for your home. You will find that your suggestiones have been included in these latest drawings.

The rooms for your childrens have been enlarged by nine square foot each. Two closets have been added in the basement.

Cleveland Landscaping Company has submitted their proposal for adding seven birch tree and five holly bushs in the backyard. I think you will be pleased with their recommendationes.

Two companys have submitted bids for paving the two driveway. Both bids are too high, and we have asked them to resubmit them. We will keep you posted on new developments.

                              Sincerely,

_____

1. _____   6. _____
2. _____   7. _____
3. _____   8. _____
4. _____   9. _____
5. _____   10. _____

Possessives

Possessives are easy to form, yet many of us confuse the spelling of possessives. Follow these guidelines:

1. For most singular words, form the possessive by adding an apostrophe (') plus *s*.

   manager/manager's   mother/mother's

   boss/boss's   Jones/Jones's   friend/friend's

2. If a singular proper name ending in *s* would be hard to pronounce with an apostrophe plus *s*, then add only the apostrophe.

   Hastings/Hastings'

3. Plural nouns ending in *s* take only an apostrophe to form their possessives.

   managers/managers'   bosses/bosses'   friends/friends'

4. Plural nouns that do not end in *s* take an apostrophe plus *s*.

   men/men's   women/women's   children/children's

5. If a compound noun is singular, add an apostrophe plus *s*.

   editor in chief/editor in chief's

6. If a compound noun is a plural ending in *s*, then add only an apostrophe.

   brigadier generals/brigadier generals'

7. If a compound noun is a plural that does not end in *s*, add an apostrophe plus *s*.

   sisters-in-law/sisters-in-law's   runners-up/runners-up's

   Notice the distinction in the use of *'s* in the following:

   Mark's and Connie's homes   Mark and Connie's homes
   (separate ownership; each noun has an *'s*)   (joint ownership; only one noun has an *'s*)

   One more rule concerning possessives: Always use a possessive form before gerunds (*ing* nouns), as shown in the following example:

   Mrs. Jonas commented on *his* arriving late to work.

● **8-4**   Proofread the following letter for errors in possessives. Circle each error, and then write the correct word or words in the space provided below the letter. (10 points each error correctly circled and 10 points each error corrected in the space provided)

Dear Mr. Mendoza:

Enclosed are three copies of the contracts for Rita R. Mendoza and Louisa L. Mendoza. This completes the necessary paperwork. Rita and Louisas Dress Shop is now ready to begin business.

Please have them sign all three copies before a notary. A notarys signature and seal are essential. Each of them should keep a copy; the third copy should be returned to me for their file.

I am sure that your sisters-in-laws shop will be successful. I know they appreciate you arranging the legal work and keeping their accounting record's.

                    Sincerely yours,

---

1. _____
2. _____
3. _____
4. _____
5. _____

● **8-5** The following memorandum has errors in spelling, plurals, and possessives. Circle each error, and write the correct word in the spaces provided. (5 points each error correctly circled and 5 points each error corrected in the space provided)

_____

MEMORANDUM

DATE   Febuary 25, 1987

TO   Fresno Company Employees

FROM   B. Harvey Dexter, Personal Manager

SUBJECT   Dental Insurance

Enclosed is a pamflet explaining Fresno Companys new dental insurence plan. This plan is open to employees, their childs, and their husbands or wifes.

Only a few companys in hour vicinity provide this coverage, and we are glad we can make it availible to you.

BHD

_____

1. _____
2. _____
3. _____
4. _____
5. _____
6. _____
7. _____
8. _____
9. _____
10. _____

Word Division

Dividing words properly at the end of a line is important for your reader. Follow these rules:

1. If possible, avoid dividing words.

2. Divide words only between syllables.

3. When in doubt about correct syllabication, check a dictionary or wordbook.

4. Do not divide one-syllable words.

5. Do not divide contractions, abbreviations, and figures.

6. Divide compound words where the two words are joined.

7. Divide hyphenated words at the hyphen.

8. Do not divide the last word on a page.

9. Ending two consecutive lines in hyphens is acceptable. Ending three or more consecutive lines in hyphens is not acceptable.

10. Do not divide a word with six or fewer letters.

11. Leave at least two letters on the line with the hyphen, and carry over at least three letters (or two letters plus a punctuation mark).

12. Divide between double consonants (unless the double consonants end the root word, as in *tell-ing, stress-ing*).

13. Divide after, not before, a single-vowel syllable (*prodi-gal*, not *prod-igal*). If there are two single-vowel syllables together, the words should be divided between these two syllables (*cre-ative*, not *crea-tive*).

14. Avoid dividing the first line and the last full line of a paragraph.

15. Try to divide a word after a prefix or before a suffix, leaving the root word undivided.

● **8-6** Using a dictionary or a wordbook as a guide, place a diagonal (/) in the following items to indicate the preferred place to divide them at the end of a typewritten or printed line. Underline any item that should not be divided. (5 points each correct answer)

1. CPA	11. anywhere
2. thirty-first	12. drilling
3. stopped	13. amiable
4. hysterical	14. rely
5. o'clock	15. dressing
6. deferred	16. splatter
7. manager	17. $12,224
8. abroad	18. $12,229.33
9. determination	19. evaluation
10. beginning	20. couldn't

● **8-7** In the following letter, some words are divided correctly; others are not. If the division is correct, write *yes* in the space provided. If the word is incorrectly divided or if dividing a word on that particular line violates one of the rules, write *no* in the space.

Dear Mr. O'Kelley: <u>Yes/No?</u>

As one of our preferred customers,
you are invited to our annual pre-inven-   1. _____
tory sale. All of our merchandise
will be reduced to the lowest possib-   2. _____
le prices to help us make room for spr-   3. _____
ing items, which are arriving daily.

The sale officially begins Monday, Janu-   4. _____
ary 15, at 10:30 a.m. However, we are
opening at 8:30 a.m.--two hours earlier--
for you, a valued charge customer. Your credit
card is your admission ticket to this super, gi-   5. _____
gantic sale.

During this two hour period--exclusively for
preferred customers--we are cutting an addi-   6. _____
tional 10 percent to give you a big incen-   7. _____
tive to shop early, save money, and take advan-   8. _____
tage of this early morning buying opportunity.

As you know, Mr. O'Kelley, our sales
have a distinct reputation for offering
the city's best bargains. You should-   9. _____
n't miss this sale! Beat the crowds and a-   10. _____
void the long lines. Come early!

           Sincerely,

Proofreading Review

● **8-A** The following letter has errors in spelling, word usage, plurals, possessives, and word division. Use proofreaders' marks to mark needed corrections.

MURDOCK'S CATALOG SHOWROOM

Post Office Box 1820
Shreveport, Louisiana 71166
(318) 555-7640

July 15, 19--

Mr. Tom Patrick
The Camera Shop, Inc.
4699 Shrank Road
Kansas City, MO 64055

Dear Tom:

Thank you for visiting our new store, Tom. It was certainly good to see you again. After all, quiet a few years have past since we were college roommates.

I am planning to add a large photography center and was impressed with your companys product line. I would appreciate your submitting a proposal by August 1. I apologize for the rush, but we have already recieved proposals from two companys.

I look forward to hearing you're ideas on this potential business venture. Thanks for takeing me to lunch.

Sincerely,

Eric Murdock

dk

● **8-B** When efficient business communicators find that they are writing essentially the same letter time after time, they develop a letter that will be appropriate with only a few minor changes each time it is used. Such a letter is called a *form letter*, and the changes are called *variables*. An example of a form letter is the collection letter written to customers who have past-due accounts. The variables in this form letter would be the amount past due and the length of time past due for each customer.

For other form letters, paragraphs can be selected from a series of form paragraphs (often called "boilerplate" paragraphs) to construct the letter. Selected parts of the letter can be changed to make the letter accurate, personal, and appropriate. The writer indicates needed changes or additions in writing or dictates them to a stenographer.

Below are six form paragraphs that the personnel manager uses to answer routine inquiries from employment applicants. Directions for constructing five letters from the form paragraphs and the five letters follow. Read the five letters that were constructed from the personnel manager's instructions. Compare the directions with the letters. Circle each error, and then answer the questions on page 100.

Form Paragraph 1

Thank you for your recent letter inquiring about employment with our company. We are pleased that you considered discussing your career plans with us.

Form Paragraph 2

You are interested in working with our __A__ department. Our staff in that department is ade- quate, and we do not anticipate an opening in the near future.

Form Paragraph 3

You are interested in working with our __B__ department. We are considering increasing the staff in that department and would like to talk with you about this opening.

Form Paragraph 4

We have scheduled an interview for you in my office at _____C_____ and hope this is a con- venient time for you to visit with us. If not, call me to arrange a more suitable time. I look forward to meeting you.

Form Paragraph 5

Your résumé would be helpful in evaluating your qualifications for the position we have available. Please mail a copy to me at your earliest convenience.

Form Paragraph 6

We appreciate your contacting us and will keep your application credentials for six months. Should we need someone with your particular expertise during that time, we will review your qualifications. At the end of six months, let us know if you want us to keep your file for consideration.

Letter   *1*

Name : *Mr. Gus Terry*   Salutation : *Dear Mr. Terry*

Address : *1232 Ahaku Place*   *¶* #   *Specific Comments:*

Honolulu, HI 96821   *1* _____

                              3   *(B) accounting*

Additional   *2:30 p.m. on*
Comments : _____   *4*   *(C) Wednesday, May 3*

_____   _____

_____   _____

Letter   1

April 25, 1988

Mr. Gus Terry
1232 Ahaku Place
Honolulu, HI 96821

Dear Mr. Terry:

Thank you for your recent letter inquiring about employment with our company. We are pleased that you considered discussing your career plans with us.

You are interested in working with our accounting department. We are considering increasing the staff in that department and would like to talk with you about this opening.

We have scheduled an interview for you in my office at 2:30 p.m. on Wednesday, May 3, and hope this is a convenient time for you to visit with us. If not, call me to arrange a more suitable time. I look forward to meeting you.

Very truly yours,

Marshall O'Keefe
Personnel Manager

dc

Letter _2_

Name : *Ms. Annette Conway*

Address : *Post Office Box 2578*
          Honolulu, HI 96803

Additional
Comments : _____

Salutation : *Dear Ms. Conway*

¶ #   *Specific Comments :*

_1_   _____

_2_   *(A) personnel*

_6_   _____

_____   _____

_____   _____

Letter 2

                                        April 25, 1988

Ms. Annette Conway
Post Office Box 2578
Honolulu, HI 96803

Dear Ms. Conway:

    Thank you for your recent letter inquiring about employment
with our company. We are pleased that you considered discussing
your career plans with us.

    You are interested in working with our personnel department.
Our staff in that department is adequate, and we do not anticipate
an opening in the near future.

    We appreciate you contacting us and will keep your application
credentials for six months. Should we need someone with your
particular expertise during that time, we will review your qualifications. At the end of six months, let us know if you want us
to keep your file for consideration.

                              Very truly yours,

                              Marshall O'Keefe
                              Personnel Manager

dc

Letter **3**

Name : *Mr. Lee Alexander*

Address : *1336 Martin Street*

Honolulu, HI 96819

Additional   ***** *It is hard to believe*
Comments : *that you will be*
graduated from college in
June. Congratulations!
****** *Please give my best*

regards to your mom and dad.

Salutation : *Dear Lee :*

¶ #   *Specific Comments :*

1   _____

*****   _____

3   *(B) engineering*

5   _____

******   _____

_____

Letter 3

April 25, 1988

Mr. Lee Alexander
1336 Martin Street
Honolulu, HI 96819

Dear Lee:

Thank you for your recent letter inquiring about employment
with our company. We are pleased that you considered discussing
your career plans with us.

It is hard to believe that you will be graduated from college
in June. Congratulations!

You are interested in working with our research department.
We are considering increasing the staff in that department and
would like to talk with you about this opening.

Your resume would be helpful in evaluating your qualifications
for the position we have available. Please mail a Copy to me at
at your convenience.

Please give my best regards to your mom and dad.

Very truly yours,

Marshall O'Keefe
Personnel Manager

dc

Letter 4

Name : *Mrs. Denise Oakland*

Address : *435 22nd Avenue*
_____ *Honolulu, HI 96818*

Additional
Comments : _____

_____

_____

Salutation : *Dear Mrs. Oakland*

¶ #   *Specific Comments:*

___ _____

 1   _____

 2   *(A) cost* _____

 6   _____

___ _____

___ _____

Letter 4

April 25, 1988

Mrs. Denise Oakland
435 22nd Avenue
Honolulu, HI 96818

Dear Mrs. Oakland:

Thank you for your recent letter inquiring about employment
with our company. We are pleased that you considered discussing
your career plans with us.

You are interested in working with our cost department. Our
staff in that department is adequate, and we do not anticipate
an opening in the near future.

We appreciate your contacting us and will keep your application
credentials for six months. Should we need someone with your
particular expertise during that time, we will review your qualifications. At the end of six months, let us know if you want us
to keep your file for consideration.

Sincerely yours,

Marshall O'Keefe
Personnel Manager

dc

Letter _5_

Name : *Mrs. Charlene Stamey*   Salutation : *Dear Mrs. Stamey*

Address : *1638 Makaiwa Street*   *¶#*   *Specific Comments:*

Honolulu, HI 96816   _1_   _____

                           _3_   *(B) word processing*

Additional   *10:30 a.m. on*
Comments : *＊Please bring a*   _4_   *(C) Thursday, May 4*

current resume with   *＊*   _____

you.   ___   _____

Letter 5

April 25, 1988

Mrs. Charlene Stamey
1638 Makaiwa Street
Honolulu, HA 96816

Dear Mrs. Stamey

   Thank you for your recent letter inquiring about employment
with our company. We are pleased that you considered discussing
your career plans with us.

   You are interested in working with our word processing
department. We are considering increasing the staff in that
department and would like to talk with you about this opening.

   We have scheduled an interview for you in my office at
9:30 a.m. on Thursday May 4, and hope this is a convenient
time for you to visit with us. If not, call me to arrange a
more suitable time. I look forward to meeting you.

   Please bring a current resume with you.

                              Very truly yours,

                              Marshall O'Keefe
                              Personnel Manager

dc

Answer the following questions in the spaces provided, identifying letters by number.

1. Which letter or letters are correct? _____

2. There is one number error in one of the five letters. Which letter contains the error? _____

3. Change _____ to _____ to correct the error.

4. Which letter contains an error in the inside address? _____

5. Change _____ to _____ to correct the error.

6. Which letter differs from the specific information within the form paragraph? _____

7. Change _____ to _____ to correct this error.

8. Which letter has a misspelled word? _____

9. Write the correct spelling _____

10. Which letter contains an error in the use of possessives? _____

11. Write the correct form. _____

12. Which letter has a repetition error? _____

13. What is repeated? _____

14. Which letter style is used for Letter 3? _____

15. Which letter has a letter format error? _____

16. Which letter has a punctuation error within a sentence? _____

17. Write the entire sentence below, correcting the punctuation and any other error.

_____

_____

_____

18. Which letter has a capitalization error? _____

19. Write the word as it should be written. _____

20. Which letter contains a spacing error? _____

21. The spacing error is between these two words: _____ and _____

22. Which letter contains a word-division error? _____

23. Where should the word be divided? _____

24. Which letter has an omission error? _____

25. What is omitted? _____

Grammar Alertness

Sentence Fragments

A complete sentence has a subject and a verb.

Our manager approved the expense. (Subject, *manager*; verb, *approved*)

Mrs. Haley and Mr. Roe are in the conference room. (Subjects, *Mrs. Haley and Mr. Roe*; verb, *are*)

Please make another copy for me. (Subject is understood to be *you—you make . . .*)

When a subject or a verb is missing, the group of words is a fragment.

Early in the morning last Tuesday. (No verb)

Some clauses may have a subject and a verb but still be incomplete.

When our supervisor arrives. (Fragment)

Because she was late this morning. (Fragment)

What will happen "When our supervisor arrives"? What happened "Because she was late this morning"? These fragments do not tell us. They are incomplete.

When our supervisor arrives, we will discuss this schedule. (Sentence)

Because she was late this morning, she missed the boss's announcement. (Sentence)

● **9-1** Which of the following items are fragments and which are sentences? Circle *S* for each complete sentence and *F* for each fragment. (10 points each item)

1. The top executives have computer terminals in their homes.   1. S   F

2. Achieving their fall-quarter goals.   2. S   F

3. Although we sold 10,000 units last year.   3. S F

4. After making 50 copies of the report which was already late.   4. S F

5. Dale Scribner is on vacation this week.   5. S F

6. Max Hempstead, who has a definite aptitude for computer programming.   6. S F

7. The manager is reading the research report at home tonight.   7. S F

8. Our company has a smoke detector system and a sprinkler system.   8. S F

9. Looking over the inventory printout and not being able to find the cases of tape.   9. S F

10. We can meet Tuesday.   10. S F

Subject-Verb Agreement

Subjects and verbs must agree. A singular subject must have a singular verb; a plural subject must have a plural verb.

My assistant is on vacation. (*Assistant,* the subject, is singular; *is,* the verb, is singular. They agree.)

My assistants are on vacation. (Here, *assistants* and *are* agree. Both are plural.)

The verbs that are most often misused in subject-verb agreement errors are *to be, to do,* and *to have.* Check a reference manual to make sure you understand how to use these verbs.

Subjects joined by *and* are plural. There are two subjects.

Mrs. Winn and Mr. Klee are here.

Two singular subjects joined by *or* need a singular verb.

Mrs. Winn or Mr. Klee is here. (Only one is here.)

When a singular and a plural subject are joined by *or,* make the verb agree with the subject closer to the verb.

Mrs. Winn or the managers have this report.
The managers or Mrs. Winn has the report.

● **9-2** Circle the correct verb. (10 points each item)

1. Roberta or Eric (was, were) selected for the management training program.

2. The invoices (was, were) keyed into the information system yesterday.

3. Most new employees (appreciate, appreciates) the orientation program.

4. The consultant and the operators (are, is) convinced that the computer system will increase efficiency.

5. New procedures (apply, applies) to everyone.

6. A case of defective fuses (was, were) returned by truck.

7. The batteries (weigh, weighs) 12 pounds each.

8. My broker (predict, predicts) that the stock value will increase.

9. Static electricity or inconsistent electrical current (are, is) causing your problem.

10. Mr. Abbott and Mr. Billingsly (are, is) here.

Parallelism

Parallelism simply means that similar constructions are treated in a similar manner. Adjectives should be parallel to adjectives, nouns to nouns, infinitives to infinitives, subordinate clauses to subordinate clauses, etc. In the examples note the words in italics.

Not Parallel

She is both *skilled* and *has experience*.

My duties include *scheduling* and *estimates*.

His hobbies are *playing* tennis and *to cook* gourmet meals.

She approved not only *my raise* but also *promoting me*.

Give copies both *to Mr. Cohn* and *Mrs. Dent*.

Parallel

She is both *skilled* and *experienced*.

My duties include *scheduling* and *estimating*.

His hobbies are *playing* tennis and *cooking* gourmet meals.

She approved not only *my raise* but also *my promotion*.

Give copies both *to Mr. Cohn* and *to Mrs. Dent*.

Parallelism is often neglected with the constructions *both ... and, either ... or, neither ... nor,* and *not only ... but also.*

● **9-3** Do the following sentences have errors in parallelism? If so, rewrite them correctly. Write *correct* in the space provided if a sentence is correct. (10 points each item)

1. At the meeting, we will elect new officers, approve departmental budgets, and to approve new procedures.

_____

_____

2. She agreed not only to attend but also addressing the seminar.

_____

_____

3. Ms. Manning's position is rewarding and a challenge.

_____

_____

4. Send letters both to Mr. Forrester and Mr. Flannigan.

_____

_____

5. Word processing equipment is fast, efficient, and expensive.

_____

_____

6. An administrative assistant is not only skilled in talking but also in listening.

_____

_____

7. Max will donate either money or to donate equipment.

_____

_____

8. Management has agreed to repair the refrigerator and paying for a microwave oven.

_____

_____

9. Crews have begun painting, papering, and to panel the walls as instructed.

_____

_____

10. Neither Miguel nor Rachel plans to apply for the position.

_____

_____

● **9-4** Use proofreaders' marks to correct sentence fragments, improper subject-verb agreement, and faulty parallelism in the following memorandum. (20 points each correction)

MEMORANDUM

Date: December 1, 1987

To: Executive Staff

From: Carl Hardin, President

Subject: Retirement Banquet

On Friday, December 15, we will honor 20 employees. Who are retiring from our company. The banquet, to be held in our recreational facilities, are scheduled for 7 p.m.

Each of these employees have 15 or more years of service with our company. We appreciate not only their hard work but also they were dedicated.

Either Donald Jay or Susan Fielding plan to represent our New York executive office. I will let you know later which one is coming. Please plan to attend the banquet.

CH

Proofreading Review

● **9-A** Proofread the following paragraphs for sentence fragments, subject-verb agreement, and parallel construction. Paragraphs may be correct or may have more than one error. Write the entire corrected paragraph in the space provided. If a paragraph has no errors, write *correct* in the space.

Paragraph 1

The customer slipped on ice in the parking lot. Until we have had a chance to investigate the incident thoroughly. We will withhold all comments.

_____

_____

_____

_____

Paragraph 2

The enclosed brochure and samples will acquaint you with our products. After you have had an opportunity to evaluate them, our sales representative will call you.

_____

_____

_____

_____

Paragraph 3

An administrative assistant handles telephone calls, makes appointments, writes letters, and to relieves the executive of routine tasks. As you can see, this position both offers variety and responsibility.

_____

_____

_____

_____

Paragraph 4

A quality communication doesn't just happen. Proofreading, editing, and revising the document is essential.

_____

_____

_____

_____

Paragraph 5

An effective executive always know what is happening in the organization. Most employees realizes this fact.

_____

_____

_____

Paragraph 6

Three clerks and the manager is going on the buying trip. All four of them has specific areas of responsibility.

_____

_____

_____

Paragraph 7

Executives must review the performance of each of their subordinates. Based on this review, the executives can recommend qualified persons for promotions.

_____

_____

_____

Paragraph 8

Each employee playing on a team must have a physical examination and qualifying for additional health and accident insurance. The company will pay for the examination and for the insurance.

_____

_____

_____

Paragraph 9

Neither George nor Fred were late this morning. They were both late yesterday. Because of car trouble.

_____

_____

_____

Paragraph 10

Mr. Sinclaire approved not only my transfer but also to promote me. I am looking forward to my new position.

_____

_____

_____

● **9-B** Before a meeting, an agenda is usually prepared. An *agenda* is a list of topics to be discussed at the meeting, often along with the names of the persons who will discuss the topics. After the meeting, minutes (or records) summarizing the discussion and listing any decisions made or actions taken at the meeting are usually typed or printed. The minutes are distributed to those who attended the meeting and other appropriate persons such as management personnel.

Proofread the agenda and the minutes that follow. Use proofreaders' marks to correct any errors that you may find.

                        Canteen Committee Meeting

                                AGENDA

                          for October 15, 19--

                      Recreation Room--10:30 A.M.

1.   Purpose of Committee

     Ted Fletcher, Assistant Manager

2.   Employee Comments

     Jill Laine

     Bill Keller

3.   Specific Problems

     Curt Goins, Canteen Manager

4.   Possible Solutions

     Ann Osacky, Personnel Manager

5.   Conclusions

                              Dale Fieldcrest
                              Discussion Leader

Canteen Committee Meeting

MINUTES

October 15, 19--

COMMITTEE   The purpose of this committee is to assess the canteen
PURPOSE   in an effort to improve it's usefulness to employees.
Ted Fletcher

Discussion: Management has received many complaints about the equipment
                   food available, and service.

EMPLOYEE   Both employee representatives on the committee expressed
COMMENTS   appreciation to management personnel for their willingness
Jill Laine   to improve the canteen.
Bill Keller

Discussion: Employees also mentioned the importance of the canteen as a
                   place to eat, take their breaks, and talking with other
                   employees.

SPECIFIC   Four main problems exist:
Problems   1. Some employees do not want smoking to be permitted in
Curt Goins   the canteen.
                   2. Food in the vending machines (particularly soup) is not
                      hot enough.
                   3. There are not enough tables and chairs during break
                      times and meal times.
                   4. Employees do not have access to a telephone during the
                      work day.

Discussion: These four main problems came to our attention through a
                   survey completed by all employees. There are other problems
                   and suggestions, but these should receive immediate
                   attention.

POSSIBLE   1. The canteen could be divided into smoking and non-smo-
SOLUTIONS   king areas.
Ann osacky   2. Our company should insist that the vending machine
                      owners have there equipment repaired. Our company
                      should buy at least one microwave oven to heat food and
                      beverages.
                   3. Management should consider staggering break and meal
                      times to eliminate overcrowding at peak times.
                   4. Two phone booths should be installed in the unused area
                      just outside the canteen.

Discussion: Many possible solutions were mentioned, but everyone agreed
                   that the solutions presented above are the most reasonable
                   and practical.

CONCLUSIONS   Ann Osacky, personnel manager, will present these ideas to
                to the executive management committee at its next meeting
                which will be within two weeks.

NEXT   Our next meeting will be november 1 at 10:30 a.m. the in
MEETING   recreation room.

                                    Dale Fieldcrest, Discussion Leader
                                    Bill Keller, Recorder

Distribution:
    Committee Members: Goins, Fletcher, Laine, Keller, Osacky, Stevens,
        and Williams
    Others: Ms. Lydia Pettus, President
             Mr. Edward Quigley, Manager

Punctuation Alertness

Periods, Colons, Exclamation Points, and Dashes

PERIODS

Use a period to end most sentences, including polite requests.

Will you please send me your check by Monday. (Not really a question)

Periods are needed in many abbreviations, but not all. (Check a comprehensive reference manual to be sure.) Be especially careful of spacing with periods in abbreviations: Ph.D., a.m., and so on.

Note that customary and metric abbreviations for weights and measurements have no periods.

12 g	14 mm	156.92 k	8 in
9 ft	22 gal		

The size of each sample should be precisely as described in the specifications: 2.5 by 3.6 by 3.9 cm.

Two-letter state abbreviations also have no periods.

IL, KS, MS, PA, WY

COLONS

The colon is used after the salutation in a business letter (Dear Ms. Cortes:) and after expressions such as *the following, as follows,* and *listed below.* The colon also introduces long quotations.

Note that the first word following a colon is capitalized (1) if that word begins a complete sentence or (2) if that word begins on a new line (as, for example, in lists).

All of us agree with John: Each estimate must be itemized so that we can be sure that the costs are accurate.

EXCLAMATION POINTS

The exclamation point is used to show strong feeling or emotion. It may be used after a complete sentence or after one word or phrase.

Beware! Dangerous chemicals are stored in this room.

She asked—again!—for overnight delivery of the entire order.

Do not overuse the exclamation point in business correspondence.

DASHES

A dash is used to make a strong break in a sentence.

One dash separates a strong comment at the end of a sentence from the rest of that sentence. An afterthought or an abrupt change in thoughts is also separated by a dash from the rest of the sentence.

We asked him to rush the check to us—by Friday, if possible.

James, Barbara, Anne, Frank—all were at the press party.

Two dashes are used if the break is in the middle of the sentence.

Only one person in our department—Vera Pulaski, our manager—knows how to use this equipment.

When used in pairs, dashes are very similar to parentheses. However, parentheses tend to deemphasize; dashes, on the other hand, tend to emphasize statements.

When typing a dash, use two hyphens with no space before, after, or between them.

● **10-1** Supply a period, colon, exclamation point, or dash in each blank space in the following letter. Leave the space empty if no punctuation is needed. (10 points each correct answer)

Mr___Oscar Standridge
Office Temporaries, Inc.___
1357 West Pueblo Drive
Pueblo, Co___ 81004

Dear Mr. Standridge___

Congratulations___ Your purchase of five Kuiper Word Processors
will give you an advantage over any temporary agency in your area___

Your word processors will be delivered August 1___ sooner if
possible. We will provide you with these services___

Equipment Installation
Staff Training
Maintenance

Productivity, efficiency, and profitability___ these are your
goals. We will help you meet them. Will you call when we can help
you further___

Parentheses, Hyphens, and Semicolons

PARENTHESES

Use parentheses to enclose:

1. Words, phrases, or clauses that are included within a sentence but are independent of the sentence.

   Ms. Nance (she is our regional sales manager) will be in the office next week.

2. Numbers or letters that enumerate items within a sentence.

   All of us agreed to (1) ..., (2) ..., and (3) ....

3. References, directions, or dates that add extra information.

   The manual clearly explains the procedure (see page 197).

   Note the following examples showing how other punctuation marks are most often used with parentheses.

   Ask Oliver (is he in today?) to help you with this project.

   Although we completed the research a long time ago (1978), we have not yet published our study.

   The present catalog lists the wrong price for electric motors (see page 145); therefore, we must correct the next printing. (In fact, we should check the prices before we reprint.)

   The last example shows how parentheses can be used to enclose an interruption within a sentence or to enclose an entire sentence. Note the capital letter for *In* and the period within the parentheses.

HYPHENS

The hyphen is most commonly used to join words—or parts of words—together. Use hyphens for all words and compound words that are hyphenated in your dictionary. In addition, use hyphens for temporary compounds—adjectives joined together to modify a noun.

   He needs a *3-inch* pipe to fix this. (*3 inches* of pipe)

   Amy has an office in a *50-story* building. (*50 stories* high)

   We bought a *low-intensity* lamp. (A lamp of *low intensity*)

   Use hyphens for fractions (two-thirds, one-half) and for numbers such as twenty-one and twenty-first.
   Also, use hyphens to show end-of-line word breaks, but follow the dictionary to make sure the breaks are correct. To save space, hyphens may be used in dates (6-5-87) in lists but not in the address line of a letter or memo.
   A hyphen may be used as follows:

   The meeting is June 10-12. (June 10 through June 12)

SEMICOLONS

The most common use of the semicolon is to join two closely related independent clauses. Usually, the second clause begins with (or includes) a word such as *therefore, however, consequently,* or *moreover.*

> He mailed the package last Friday; therefore, we should surely receive it by tomorrow.

> Mrs. Anson refused to increase our expense budget; she suggested, moreover, that we decrease it by 10 percent.

Note the pattern of comma use with *therefore* and *moreover.*

The semicolon replaces the comma in a series when one or more of the items in the series already includes a comma.

> She will be traveling to Kansas City, Kansas; Austin, Texas; Charlotte, North Carolina; and Gardiner, Massachusetts.

The three semicolons help to separate these four items; commas would merely add to the confusion.

● **10-2** Supply the needed parentheses, hyphens, and semicolons in the following memorandum. In some cases, you will have to change existing punctuation. (10 points each correctly inserted hyphen, semicolon, and pair of parentheses)

MEMORANDUM

To: Mildred Berstein   From: Stan Cosby

Subject: Promotions and Transfers   Date: April 20, 1987

Three employees have been approved for promotion and transfer. These criteria see page 168 of the company policy manual were used in select ing the branch managers: (1) qualifications, (2) seniority, and 3 job performance.

The branch managers and their new locations are as follows: Stephen Delanta, Houston, Texas, Edith Boudreaux, Atlanta, Georgia, and J. B. Cohn, Sacramento, California. These new managers represent about thirty two years of sales experience.

The managers may assume their new positions as early as June 1 however, they must report by July 1. Fred Harbinger he is our relocation specialist will help make the move as smooth as possible.

Each of the new managers should plan to attend the executive level conference to be held May 15 17 in St. Louis, Missouri. Conference details will be available next week.

                        SC

dk

Question Marks, Quotation Marks, and Underscores

QUESTION MARKS

A question mark may be used at the end of a sentence or at the end of a parenthetical comment within a sentence.

> Will the analysis be ready by June 12?

> The analysis (will it be ready by June 12?) will help us to interpret these figures.

QUOTATION MARKS

Use quotation marks to enclose a person's exact words.

> "We are on schedule," she said. "In addition, we are within the expense budget."

Commas and periods are always placed inside quotation marks, as in the above example. Colons and semicolons are placed outside quotation marks. Exclamation points and question marks may go inside or outside the second quotation mark, depending on whether the mark belongs with the quoted words only or with the entire sentence.

> Why didn't you mark this "Fragile"? (The question mark belongs to the entire sentence, not just the quoted word.)

> She specifically said, "Fred, will you be at the meeting?" (The question mark belongs with the quoted words.)

Use quotation marks for parts of books, magazines, or other published works.

> The last chapter, "How to Supervise People," is the most interesting chapter in *Successful Management.*

UNDERSCORES

Words used as words are usually underscored.

> Throughout this report, the word receive is misspelled.

> The term psychosomatic has an interesting derivation.

Titles of books, plays, and other complete works are underscored or they may be typed in solid capital letters.

> Three of Mary Stewart's best books are The Crystal Cave, The Hollow Hills, and The Last Enchantment.

In letters, the attention line and subject line are either underscored or typed in solid capital letters.

> Attention: Ms. Edna Austin

Underscores provide emphasis in typewritten materials. In printed material, *italic type* is usually used for emphasis.

● **10-3** Supply question marks, quotation marks, and underscores in the following memorandum. (20 points each question mark, underscore, or pair of quotation marks correctly placed)

MEMORANDUM

DATE: October 20, 1987

TO: Tammy Rikard, Administrative Assistant

FROM: Jesse Robilard, Office Manager

SUBJECT: Subscriptions to <u>Office Choices</u>

Did you subscribe to the magazine, Office Choices, for our staff Art Brackston, who conducted our last office management training session, said, This magazine should be required reading for all office employees.

Attached is another excellent article that I clipped from the magazine. This particular article, Implementing Information Processing, addresses the term cyberphobia, which is the fear of computers.

Let's talk about the article after you have had a chance to read it.

                 JR

cw
Enclosure

● **10-4** Proofread the following sentences. Use proofreaders' marks to insert, delete, change, or move punctuation as necessary. (10 points each correction)

1. Each issue of the magazine has up to date information.

2. Did you mark the package "Special Delivery?"

3. The word mistake has a negative connotation.

4. Some years ago about 1982 we investigated the claim.

5. "We plan to expand our business", reported the company president.

6. The cases, weighing 110 kg each, were shipped yesterday.

7. The controller asked, "Will the report be ready by Friday"?

8. Jill excitedly announced, "Our idea was accepted"!

9. What is your flight schedule?

10. Francisco, Jim, and Della all of them applied for the job.

Proofreading Review

● **10-A** Assuming that the punctuation already typed in the following application letter is correct, supply the omitted punctuation.

                                        Campus Box 748
                                        City University
                                        Shelby, NC 28150
                                        April 25, 19--

Mrs. Gail Bracken
Personnel Officer
First Bank, Inc.
Charlotte, NC 28206

Dear Mrs. Bracken

    Can First Bank, Inc., use a hard working young man who is looking
for an accounting oriented career I feel that my education and personal
qualities qualify me for the accounting trainee position you advertised
in the April 22 Charlotte Observer.

    As a college senior, my experience in banking is limited
however my willingness to work hard is unlimited. Each of my jobs has
involved direct contact with people. My job as a camp counselor taught
me patience in dealing with others. My business communications class
and my human behavior class have helped me realize the importance of
relationships inside and outside the organization.

    I took my education seriously and also found time to get involved
with campus activities. My 3.8 average (4.0 scale is an indication of
the emphasis placed on education. Realizing that a college education
does not take place entirely in the classroom, I became involved in
campus activities. Dressing up in a bulldog suit, mingling with the
crowds, attending charitable functions these were a few of my
responsibilities after being elected school mascot. Being captain of
the soccer team and president of the student body demonstrate my
leadership ability.

    You advertised for "an aggressive, organized individual with
strong human relations skills. May I have an interview to personally
demonstrate my qualifications My résumé is enclosed. Please write me
or call me at (704) 555-4938.

                                        Sincerely,

                                        Ben H. Michaels

Enclosure

● **10-B** Use proofreaders' marks to indicate errors in the following résumé. Assume that the existing punctuation is correct.

BEN H. MICHAELS

Home Address
Post Office Box 2839
Charlotte, NC 28206
(704) 555-2948

Campus Address
Campus Box 748
City University
Shelby NC 28150
(704) 555-6729

POSITION
OBJECTIVE
An entry level position in accounting, finance, or auditing that offers opportunity for advancement.

EDUCATION
Bachelor of Science Degree with a major in accounting from City University expected May 10, 19--. Grade Point Average is 3.8 on a 4.0 scale. Graduating in top 5% of the class.

Representative Courses

Major Courses	Related Courses
Accounting Principles	Business Calculus
Intermediate Accounting	Statistics
Advanced Business Law	Business Communicatins
Federal Income Tax	Human Behavior
Federal Income Tax (Advanced)	Computer Principles
Advanced Accounting	BASIC Programming
Auditing	COBOL Programming
CPA Reveiw	Microcomputer Accounting

WORK
EXPERIENCE

Summer Employment

1986   Head Cashier, Mamas Pizza Parlor, Charlotte, NC
1985   Arts and Crafts Director, Mountain Summer Camp, Kings Mountain, NC
1984   Cook, Campus Diner, Shelby, NC

Work-Study Employment

1986   Supervisor, Student Accounting Lab
1985   Tudor, College Algebra

HONORS
1982 86 Dean's List (Four Years
1986   Presidential Assistant

ORGANIZATIONS
Phi beta Lambda   Concert Choir
Student Government Association   Pep Band
Soccer Team

HOBBYS
Jogging, reading, swimming, and to ride horseback

REFERENCES AND
TRANSCRIPTS
References and transcripts will be furnished on request.

Proofreading Statistical and Technical Documents

Much of what is keyboarded today involves numbers and specialized terms. This can be attributed somewhat to our technological age. Numbers and terms must be correct in documents. A decimal, for example, can make a big difference in an invoice amount. Suppose you invoiced someone $55.97 instead of $559.70 for a stereo system. If the error is not found and corrected, your company would lose $503.73.

Some documents combine text, numbers, and specialized terms; this is indeed a challenge to the proofreader. Here are some pointers for proofreading such documents:

▼▼ Proofreading Pointers

▼ When keyboarding tabulated lists, add a blank line of space every three to five items. This makes reading and proofreading easier.

▼ Verify questionable content by checking an appropriate source.

▼ Make a list of each new or unfamiliar term (include correct spelling and definition) encountered on the job.

▼ Proofread each part—text, statistics, and technical terms—as a separate step.

▼ Proofread letter by letter, character by character, and so on.

▼ Even though you are concentrating on figures, terms, and details, remember to proofread for content and for format.

▼ Check for alignment errors when proofreading tabulated lists. For example, decimals should be under decimals and commas under commas.

▼ Verify any calculations, such as extensions on invoices and totals on financial documents.

▼ When possible, use a partnership approach to proofreading. This means that one person reads aloud from the draft as a second person verifies the final copy.

▼ Slide a ruler down the page, line by line, to keep eyes focused on the correct line.

▼ Avoid proofreading statistical and technical documents for long periods of time. This kind of proofreading is tiring; therefore, this task should be interspersed with other office jobs.

● **11-1** Proofread the following items. Write *S* for *same* if all columns are identical. If one column is different, write its letter, *A*, *B*, or *C*, in the space provided. (10 points for each correct answer)

A	B	C	
1. XL-24817	XL-24877	XL-24817	1. _____
2. laissez-faire	laissez-faire	laissez-faire	
nonsequitur	nonsequitur	nonseguitur	2. _____
3. $22,346.25	$22,346.25	$22,346.25	
<u>21,214.50</u>	<u>21,21.450</u>	<u>21,214.50</u>	
$43,560.75	$43,560.75	$43,560.75	3. _____
4. TL-4657-A	TL-4657-A	TL-4657-A	
AL-4132-D	AL-4132-D	AL-4132-D	
RT-4241-F	RT-4241-F	RT-4241-F	
XC-6155-R	XC-6155-R	XC-6155-R	
TL-5141-L	TE-5141-L	TE-5141-L	4. _____
5. pro rata	pro rata	pro rata	
modus operandi	modus operandi	modus operandi	
alma mater	alma mater	alma mater	5. _____
6. appendix	appendix	appendix	
appendixes	appendixes	appendixes	
appendices	appendices	appendices	6. _____
7. H_2O	H_2O	H_2O	
H_2SO_4	H_2SO_4	H_2SO_4	
NaCl	NaCl	NaCl	
$C_5H_{11}NO_2S$	$C_5H_{11}NO_2S$	$C_5H_{11}NO_2S$	7. _____
8. 60,232.46518	60,232.45618	60,232.46518	
80,521.00412	80,521.00412	80,521.00412	
98,452.26148	98,542.26148	98,452.26148	8. _____

	A	B	C
9.	appendectomy	appendectomy	appendectony
	tonsillectomy	tonsillectomy	tonsillectomy
	penicillin	penicillin	penicillin
10.	simultaneous output	simultaneous output	simultaneous output
	bidirectional printers	bidirectional printers	bidirectional printers
	dual-density diskette	dual-density diskette	dual-density diskette
	peripheral	peripheral	peripheral

9. _____

10. _____

● **11-2** Below is a handwritten list of used cars that is the basis for the letter that follows. Assuming that the handwritten list is correct, use proofreaders' marks to correct the errors in the letter. Put a small check beside each line in the tabulated list that is correct. (10 points each line correctly marked)

LIST OF CARS TO BE CLEANED

Pontiac	Chevrolet	Mercury
HT-6293B-772V	Nova	1981
Firebird	FR-49363-542K	Cougar
1983	1983	92,487
74,889	79,245	PZ-82863-438R

Ford	Ford	Honda
WR-48299-887J	WR-49277-665L	1986
Bronco	Thunderbird	QS-67881-994P
1984	1985	29,486
61,425	22,479	Civic

Chrysler	Dodge	Oldsmobile
YD-57293-628C	Omni	Cutlas
Imperial	RW-24832-682M	FH-62839-332Y
89,442	42,226	39,285
1982	1986	1985

Buick
SL-34240-328H
Regal
1983
52,449

BUD'S USED CARS
2697 Fillmore Boulevard   Ogden, Utah 97302
(503) 555-2940

March 29, 1987

Mr. Craig Mitchell
Automobile Cleaning Service
Post Office Box 2849
Ogden, UT 97302

Dear Craig:

Below is a list of the used cars that we are sending you for cleaning.
Each one will be personally delivered to your cleaning service by one
of our drivers.

Make	Model	Serial Number	Year	Mileage
Buick	Regal	SL-34240-328H	1984	52,449
Chevrolet	Nova	FR-49363-542K	1983	79,245
Chrysler	Imperial	YD-57293-628G	1982	89,442
Dodge	Omni	RW-248320682M	1986	42,226
Ford	Bronco	WR-48299-887J	1984	61,425
Ford	Thunderbird	WR-49277-665L	1985	22,497
Honda	Civic	QS-67881-994P	1986	29,486
Mercury	Cougar	PZ-82863-438R	1981	92,487
Oldsmobile	Cutlas	FH-72839-332Y	1985	39,285
Pontiac	Firebird	HT-62938-772V	1983	74,889

Please clean them as usual--interior and exterior. As mentioned in our
phone call, I have agreed to pay your customary charge of $200 per
vehicle.

                    Sincerely,

                    Marsha D. Segal

vt

● **11-3** Your company is printing a cookbook as a project to raise money for a local charity. Below are three recipes that will be included. Assume that the handwritten copies are correct. Use revision symbols to mark the errors in the printed copy. (20 points each error correctly marked)

Quick Biscuits

Mix together:

2 c self-rising flour   4 tbsp mayonnaise
1 tsp sugar   1 c sweet milk or buttermilk

Pour mixture into 12 lightly greased muffin tins. Bake 10 minutes at 475°.

Quick Mixed-Vegetable Casserole

Mix these ingredients and put them into a casserole dish:

2 cans mixed vegetables (drained)
1 c shredded cheddar cheese
1 c mayonnaise
1 can water chestnuts (drained and diced)

Mix these ingredients and put them on top of the casserole:

24 Saltines (crushed)
½ stick margarine or butter (melted)

Bake casserole at 350° for 30 minutes.

Miniature Cheesecakes

Mix these ingredients:

2 8-oz packages cream cheese   ¾ c sugar
1 tbsp lemon juice   2 eggs
1 tsp vanilla extract

Line miniature cupcake tins with paper liners. Place one vanilla wafer in the bottom of each liner. Spoon the above mixture into the liners.

Bake 20 minutes at 350°. Let the cheesecakes cool and remove the liners. Add one small spoon of cherry pie filling to the top of each cake.

Quick Biscuits

Mix together:

> 2 c flour
> 4 tbsp mayonnaise
> 1 c sweet milk or buttermilk
> 1 tsp sugar

Pour mixture into 12 lightly greased muffin tins. Bake 100 minutes at 475°.

Mixed-Vegetable Casserole

Mix these ingredients and put them into a casserole dish:

> 2 cans mixed vegetables (drained)
> 1 c shredded cheddar cheese
> 1 c mayonnaise
> 1 can water chestnuts (drained and diced)

Mix these ingredients and put them on top of the casserole:

> 24 Saltines (crushed)
>
> ½ stick margarine or butter (melted)

Bake casserole at 550° for 30 minutes.

Miniature Cheesecakes

Mix these ingredients:

> 2 8-oz packages cream cheese
> 3/4 c sugar
> 2 eggs
> 1 tbsp lemon juice
> 1 tbsp vanilla extract

Line miniature cupcake tins with paper liners. Place one vanilla wafer in the bottom of each liner. Spoon the above mixture into the liners.

Bake 20 minutes at 350°. Let the cheesecakes cool and remove the liners. Add one small spoonful of cherry pie filling to the top of each cake.

Proofreading Review

● **11-A** You work for The Tire Specialist, 2418 East Dixon Boulevard, Shelby, North Carolina 28150, telephone number (704) 555-7602, and store hours are 7:30 a.m. to 7:30 p.m. Monday through Saturday.

    Below is a handwritten list of tires that you want to advertise as special sale items for your annual vacation sale. The sale will run from May 25 to May 30. Also below is the proof for the ad that will appear in your local newspaper. Proofread the ad, marking any needed changes.

SUPER SAVER RADIALS

185/80R13	$39.95
185/75R14	$49.95
195/75R14	$50.95
205/75R15	$55.95
215/75R15	$65.95
225/75R15	$69.95

SUPER SAFETY RADIALS

195/70R13	$59.95
205/70R14	$65.95
215/70R14	$69.95
225/70R15	$79.95

ULTRA RADIALS

225/75R15	$85.95
235/75R15	$89.95
275/75R15	$99.95

ANNUAL VACATION SPECIAL
May 25 — May 30

SUPER SAVER RADIALS

185/80R13	$39.95
185/75R14	$49.95
195/75R14	$50.95
215/75R15	$55.95
215/75R15	$65.95
225/75R15	$69.95

SUPER SAFETY RADIALS

195/70R13	$59.95
205/70R14	$65.95
215/70R14	$69.95
225/70R15	$97.95

ULTRA RADIALS

225/75R15	$85.95
225/75R15	$89.95
275/95R15	$99.95

See ***The Tire Specialist***

2418 East Dixon Boulevard
Shelby, North Carolina 28150
(704) 555-8602

7:30 a.m. to 7:30 p.m.
Monday–Saturday

● **11-B** Below is a handwritten purchase request. Compare it with the purchase orders that were prepared based on the request. Use proofreaders' marks to correct any errors in the purchase orders. If a purchase order is correct, sign your name in the blank provided beside *Purchasing Agent*.

FROM THE DESK OF **Bill Chapin**

Lisa,
Please order the following items from Safety Equipment and Supply, Post Office Box 24815, Amarillo, TX 79106:

10
Polyethylene Molded Hard Hat
Red
$4
17-01246

20
Earplugs (30" Cord)
Black
$1
12-00587

10
Soft Frame Safety Goggles
Black
$3
10-00621

5
Pocket Case Thermometer
Chrome
$8
15-04621

MONTVUE MANUFACTURING COMPANY, INC.
2218 Industrial Boulevard Amarillo, TX 79106
(806) 555-3410

Purchase Order No. 2183

To: Safety Equipment and Supply
Post Office Box 24815
Amarillo, TX 79106

Date: 2/5/--

Ship Via:

PLEASE SHIP AND BILL US FOR THE GOODS LISTED BELOW. IF FOR ANY REASON YOU CANNOT DELIVER WITHIN 30 DAYS, LET US KNOW AT ONCE. PLEASE REFER TO OUR PURCHASE ORDER NUMBER (ABOVE) IN ALL COMMUNICATIONS.

QUANTITY	DESCRIPTION	YOUR CAT. NO.	UNIT PRICE	AMOUNT
10	Polythylene Molded Hard Hat, Red	17-01246	$4	$40.00
10	Soft Frame Safety Goggles, Black	10-00621	$3	$30.00
20	Earplugs, Black	12-00587	$1	$20.00
15	Pocket Case Thermometer, Chrome	15-04621	$8	$40.00
	Total			$130.00

NOTE: YOUR BILL TO US SHOULD INDICATE ALL YOUR USUAL DISCOUNTS. PAYMENT WILL BE MADE UPON RECEIPT OF BILL WITH GOODS. _____ Purchasing Agent

Lisa,
Please order the following items from Industrial Supply,
Inc., Post Office Box 23216, Amarillo, TX 79106:

1 Utility Exhaust Fan, Black, $75, 21-03984-K
5 Super Safety Gloves (Women's), White, $1, 27-00345-W
5 Super Safety Gloves (Men's), White, $1, 27-00345-M

ONTVUE MANUFACTURING COMPANY, INC.
2218 Industrial Boulevard   Amarillo, TX 79106
(806) 555-3410

Purchase Order No. 2184

To: Industrial Supply, Inc.
Post Office Box 23216
Amarillo, TX 79106

Date: 2/5/--

Ship Via:

PLEASE SHIP AND BILL US FOR THE GOODS LISTED BELOW.
IF FOR ANY REASON YOU CANNOT DELIVER WITHIN 30 DAYS,
LET US KNOW AT ONCE. PLEASE REFER TO OUR PURCHASE
ORDER NUMBER (ABOVE) IN ALL COMMUNICATIONS.

QUANTITY	DESCRIPTION	YOUR CAT. NO.	UNIT PRICE	AMOUNT
1	Utility Exhaust Fan, Black	21-03984-K	$75	$75.00
5	Super Safety Gloves (Womens), White	27-00345-W	$1	$15.00
5	Super Safety Gloves (Men's), White	27-00345-M	$1	$5.00
	Total			$85.00

NOTE: YOUR BILL TO US SHOULD INDICATE ALL YOUR USUAL DIS-
COUNTS. PAYMENT WILL BE MADE UPON RECEIPT OF BILL WITH GOODS. _____ Purchasing Agent

FROM THE DESK OF Bill Chapin

Lisa,
Please order the following supplies from Granberg's
Office Supply Inc., Post Office Box 44392, Amarillo, TX 79106:
2
Waste Receptacles, 15" x 23", Beige
$50
HL 61543
5
Cushioned Floor Mat, 3' x 10', Tweed
$40
RF-89161
2
Commercial Electric Wall Clock, Beige
$20
NL-64132

MONTVUE MANUFACTURING COMPANY, INC.
2218 Industrial Boulevard Amarillo, TX 79106
(806) 555-3410

Purchase Order No. 2185

To: Granberg's office Supply, Inc.
Post Office Box 44932
Amarillo, TX 79106

Date: 2/5/--

Ship Via:

PLEASE SHIP AND BILL US FOR THE GOODS LISTED BELOW.
IF FOR ANY REASON YOU CANNOT DELIVER WITHIN 30 DAYS,
LET US KNOW AT ONCE. PLEASE REFER TO OUR PURCHASE
ORDER NUMBER (ABOVE) IN ALL COMMUNICATIONS.

QUANTITY	DESCRIPTION	YOUR CAT. NO.	UNIT PRICE	AMOUNT
2	Waste Receptacles (15" x 23"), Beige	HL-61543	$50	$100.00
5	Cushioned Floor Mat (3" x 10"), Tweed	BF-89161	$40	$200.00
2	Commercial Electric Wall Clock, Beige	NL-64132	$20	$40.00
	Total			$440.00

NOTE: YOUR BILL TO US SHOULD INDICATE ALL YOUR USUAL DIS-
COUNTS. PAYMENT WILL BE MADE UPON RECEIPT OF BILL WITH GOODS. _____ Purchasing Agent

Correcting

Inconsistencies

An experienced business communicator or other office professional should be skilled in detecting inconsistencies. In most cases, inconsistencies are simply the result of treating similar items differently. However, being consistent involves much more.

Under the label *inconsistency,* we will include the following kinds of writing errors:

1. Treating similar things differently.
   a. *Formats:* Using two different letter formats; for example, indenting one paragraph in a letter when all other paragraphs are not indented.
   b. *Phone numbers:* Using two different styles; for example, (803) 555-2718 and 803-555-2718.
   c. *Dates in tables:* Using two different styles; for example, 11-21-87 and 11/21/87.
   d. *Book titles:* Using two different styles; for example, THIRD WAVE and Third Wave.
   e. *Numbers:* Mixing spelled-out numbers and figures in the same sentence; for example, nine researchers and 14 conferences.
   f. *Abbreviations:* Mixing an abbreviation and a spelled-out term—such as *gallons* and *gal*—in the same sentence.
   g. *Spelling:* Spelling someone's name two ways; for example, *Lynn* and *Lynne.*
   h. *Courtesy titles:* Using two different courtesy titles— such as *Ms.* and *Dr.*— for the same person.
   i. *Punctuation style:* Using two different comma styles—such as *Dennis Garner, Jr.,* and *Dennis Garner Jr.*—in the same communication. (The comma here is neither "right" nor "wrong" but a matter of Mr. Garner's preference.)

2. Conveying unintentional bias.
   a. *Names and other lists:* Use alphabetical order. Some readers may assume that someone or something is more important because it is first on the list. Often this is true because a writer prioritizes items in a list without a conscious awareness that this is being done. A deliberate alphabetizing

reduces the possibility of conveying unintentional bias (for instance, Berstrom, Kline, Werner; Atlanta, New York, and St. Louis).

b. *Men and women:* Treat the names of men and women alike. Omit the *Ms.* in the following example:
Alvin Berstrom, *Ms.* Launita Kline, and Bill Werner

3. Making sequencing errors. The following examples could be improved with appropriate sequencing;
   a. *Alphabetical:* Wilson, Anderson, and Tewilliger.
   b. *Chronological order:* June 5, July 10, and April 5.
   c. *Numerical order:* Check 102, Check 103, and Check 101.

4. Overlooking contradictions.
   a. *Math calculations:* You paid $30 of your $50 bill, which leaves an unpaid balance of $10. (Should be $20)
   b. *Fact:* The speed limit increases from 45 mph to 35 mph in residential areas. (Should be *decreases*)
   c. *Calendar:* Please call me Friday, May 6. (Verify that Friday is the 6th of May)

As you can see from these examples, inconsistencies can occur easily in business writing. A word of caution—the list above contains only examples. You will find other inconsistencies in exercises in this book and in the business world.

You will learn that some inconsistencies are noticed only during the second reading of a document. Others can be spotted more easily by *scanning* (looking over) the copy either before or after it is read word for word. The use of two different letter formats, for example, may be more obvious when the letter is scanned than when it is read word for word.

Like many other skills, expert proofreading is developed only through practice. The next exercises will help you spot inconsistencies.

▼▼ Proofreading Pointers

▼ Scan a document before reading it to find obvious errors such as formatting errors.

▼ Inconsistencies are easier to spot if you proofread similar items in a separate step; for example, proofread all tables in a document together.

● **12-1** If there are inconsistencies in the following items, circle them and write *yes* in the space provided. If the item has no inconsistencies, write *no* in the space. (10 points each correct item)

Yes/No?

1. Dr. Walter Durango will be our consultant. Mr. Durango

   has much experience in dealing with problems like ours.   1. _____

Yes/No?

2. We received 25 pounds of dye today and 15 lbs yesterday.   2. _____

3. Mrs. Ann McDonald will arrive at 2 p.m. today. Will you please meet Mrs. MacDonald at the airport.   3. _____

4. Computer disks are on sale this week. We can buy 12 for $10 instead of $15. This is a saving of $10.   4. _____

5. The first invoice was dated May 10, 1987; the second one was dated May 15, 1987.   5. _____

6. Should Ben be transferred to Houston, Dallas, or Fort Worth?   6. _____

7. They have paid these invoices: 2146, 2147, and 2145.   7. _____

8. Send copies of all correspondence to Milton Ibriham, Dwight Mostello, and Mrs. Linda Speldman.   8. _____

9. We hired 12 word processing operators, two proofreaders, and one administrative assistant.   9. _____

10. Our company has two phone numbers: (916) 555-8629 and 916-555-8639.   10. _____

● **12-2** Assume that the calendar below is correct for the current year.

S M T W T F S	S M T W T F S	S M T W T F S	S M T W T F S
JAN	**APR**	**JULY**	**OCT**
1 2 3 4 5 6 7	1	1	1 2 3 4 5 6 7
8 9 10 11 12 13 14	2 3 4 5 6 7 8	2 3 4 5 6 7 8	8 9 10 11 12 13 14
15 16 17 18 19 20 21	9 10 11 12 13 14 15	9 10 11 12 13 14 15	15 16 17 18 19 20 21
22 23 24 25 26 27 28	16 17 18 19 20 21 22	16 17 18 19 20 21 22	22 23 24 25 26 27 28
29 30 31	23 24 25 26 27 28 29	23 24 25 26 27 28 29	29 30 31
	30	30 31	
FEB	**MAY**	**AUG**	**NOV**
1 2 3 4	1 2 3 4 5 6	1 2 3 4 5	1 2 3 4
5 6 7 8 9 10 11	7 8 9 10 11 12 13	6 7 8 9 10 11 12	5 6 7 8 9 10 11
12 13 14 15 16 17 18	14 15 16 17 18 19 20	13 14 15 16 17 18 19	12 13 14 15 16 17 18
19 20 21 22 23 24 25	21 22 23 24 25 26 27	20 21 22 23 24 25 26	19 20 21 22 23 24 25
26 27 28	28 29 30 31	27 28 29 30 31	26 27 28 29 30
MAR	**JUNE**	**SEPT**	**DEC**
1 2 3 4	1 2 3	1 2	1 2
5 6 7 8 9 10 11	4 5 6 7 8 9 10	3 4 5 6 7 8 9	3 4 5 6 7 8 9
12 13 14 15 16 17 18	11 12 13 14 15 16 17	10 11 12 13 14 15 16	10 11 12 13 14 15 16
19 20 21 22 23 24 25	18 19 20 21 22 23 24	17 18 19 20 21 22 23	17 18 19 20 21 22 23
26 27 28 29 30 31	25 26 27 28 29 30	24 25 26 27 28 29 30	24 25 26 27 28 29 30
			31

Today is April 3. Proofread the following letter word for word, and then scan it. List the line number and the inconsistencies in the spaces provided. (20 points for each inconsistency identified)

CITY
CIVIC
SOCIETY

Post Office Box 4629   Wilmington, Delaware 19810   (302) 555-3470

1

April 3, 19--

Dr. Alfredo Alberghetti   2
3325 Hermitage Road   3
Wilmington, Delaware 19810   4

Dear Mr. Alberghetti: 5

Thank you for agreeing to speak at next month's staff   6
meeting. As you know, we meet the first Monday night   7
of each month at 7 a.m. in our hospital's auditorium.   8

We are eager to hear the results of the patient survey that   9
was conducted during the last two months. Mr. Warren Troy, 10
your researcher, said that her findings were significant.   11

Mr. Troy also mentioned that 850 of the 950 people surveyed 12
responded. This is a high percentage of response; only 200 13
people did not return the questionnaire.   14

Your presentation should take about 40 minutes. Please let 15
us know if you need any special equipment such as projectors 16
or screens. As mentioned earlier, you and I will have dinner 17
after this June 1 presentation.   18

Sincerely,   19

Haskel R. Demetri   20
Speaker's Bureau Manager

dk

---

1. Line _____ conflicted with Line _____.

   _____ conflicted with _____

2. Line _____ conflicted with line _____.

   _____ conflicted with _____

3. Line _____ conflicted with Line _____.

   _____ conflicted with _____

4. Line _____ conflicted with Line _____.

   _____ conflicted with _____

5. Line _____ conflicted with Line _____.

   _____ conflicted with _____

● **12-3** Proofread the following memo word for word, and then scan it. In the space provided, list the line number of each inconsistency, the inconsistency, and the reason you consider it an inconsistency. Refer to the calendar on page 130. (20 points for each inconsistency correctly identified)

MEMORANDUM

DATE:	April 5, 1987	1
TO:	Jake Pratersburg, Personnel Assistant	2
FROM:	Amy Oldenstern, Personnel Manager	3
SUBJECT:	New Employees	4

Below is a list of our new employees and the information required   5
by our insurance company, Accident and Health Specialists of Chicago.   6
Please send this information to them as soon as possible.   7

Name	Social Security Number	Date Employed	Date of Birth	Type of Coverage	
					8
					9
					10
J. Martin Durham	326-87-2818	4-3-87	7/15/56	Employee/Spouse	11
Daniel K. Enslow	294-56-8921	4-1-87	1/26/40	Employee/Spouse	12
Christina Jones	415-89-2371	4-2-87	11-13-30	Family	13
Elisa T. Ogden	217-52-2941	4-2-87	12/16/66	Employee Only	14
F. Simpson Weinberg	227-61-3847	4-3-87	3/21/95	Family	15

    Thank you.   16

                       AO   17

fg   18

cc: Malado, Bellini, and Sarto   19

1. Line number _____

   Inconsistency _____

   Reason _____

2. Line number _____

   Inconsistency _____

   Reason _____

3. Line number _____

   Inconsistency _____

   Reason _____

4. Line number _____

   Inconsistency _____

   Reason _____

5. Line number _____

   Inconsistency _____

   Reason _____

Proofreading Review

● **12-A** It is your job to balance the petty cash on Monday of each week. When an employee spends petty cash, he or she prepares a voucher, places the voucher in the cash box, and takes the cash that was spent. Attached to the voucher is a receipt, such as a sales slip, to verify how much money was spent.

   Examine the petty cash summary below and the vouchers and receipts that follow. You began the month with $75, and you have $31.16 on hand. The petty cash summary (based on the vouchers) indicates that you should have $31.16 on hand. However, compare each voucher with the corresponding receipt. Assume that the receipts are correct. Then compare the vouchers and receipts with the entries in the petty cash summary. If the voucher is correct, write *yes* in the space provided below. If there is an error, correct it.

1. Voucher 41 _____ If not, what is the correct amount? _____

2. Voucher 42 _____ If not, what is the correct amount? _____

3. Voucher 43 _____ If not, what is the correct amount? _____

4. Voucher 44 _____ If not, what is the correct amount? _____

5. Voucher 45 _____ If not, what is the correct amount? _____

6. To whom do you owe money, and how much do you owe to each?

   _____

   _____

   _____

7. Strike through any incorrect amount on the petty cash summary, and write the correct amount beside it.

Petty Cash Summary

Beginning Balance November 13, 19--		$75.00
Postage Expense	$12.75	
Postage Expense	.58	
Office Supplies Expense	9.99	
Subscriptions Expense	8.70	
Entertainment Expense	11.82	
		43.84
Balance on Hand November 20, 19--		$31.16

No. _41_   Amount $ _12.75_

PETTY CASH VOUCHER

Paid to _U.S. Post Office_

Charge to _Postage Expense_

For _Special Delivery_

By _Fred Landers_
_11/14/--_

U.S. Post Office

RECEIVED
11/14/--

$12.75
LMJ

No. _42_   Amount $ 8 $\frac{70}{}$

PETTY CASH VOUCHER

Paid to _Carrier, Evening Star News_____

Charge to _Subscriptions Expense_____

For _November Subscription_____

By _Linda Horne_____
11/14/--

**RECEIPT BOOK FOR
EVENING STAR NEWS**

Date _11/14/--_

Subscriptions:

Year: _____

Month: _November -- $8.70_____

Week: _____

Carrier _Lee Andrews_

Subscriber:

_Office Services, Inc._____

_Turner Building_____

_____

SCRATCH PAD

S
C
R
A
T
C
H

P
A
D

_I received 85¢
postage due from
Sarah Langston._

Anne Dempsey
11/16/--

No. _43_   Amount $ .58

PETTY CASH VOUCHER

Paid to _Mail Carrier -- Anne Dempsey_____

Charge to _Postage Expense_____

For _Postage due on package from King Brothers____

By _Sarah Langston_____
11/16/--

No. _44_   Amount $ _11.82_

PETTY CASH VOUCHER

Paid to _Bernie's Grocery_____

Charge to _Entertainment Expense_____

For _Board of Directors Meeting_____

5 lb coffee	$6.49	
Cream	1.89	By _Bill Frady_
2 lb sugar	1.10	_11/17/--_
3 doz cups	1.98 = $11.46 + .36 = $11.82	

No. _45_   Amount $ _9.99_

PETTY CASH VOUCHER

Paid to _Pendergrass Office Supply_____

Charge to _Office Supplies Expense_____

For _____

Tape	$2.29	
Lables	$1.95	By _Ruth O'Grady_
Envelopes	$5.75 = $9.99	_11/20/--_

CASH REGISTER TAPE

00	
6.49	
1.89	
1.10	
1.98	
11.46	Subtotal
.46	Tax
11.92	Total

Date _11/18_ 19 _--_

Name _Ruth O'Grady_

Address _Office Services, Turner Building_

Quantity	Description	Price	Amount
1	Roll Tape	$2.29	$2.29
1	Package Labels	$1.95	$1.95
1	Box Envelopes	$5.75	$5.75
			$9.99
		Tax	40
		Total	$10.39

All claims and returned goods must be accompanied by this bill.

No. _92_   Received by _RLT_

● **12-B** Compare the handwritten draft with the printed copy. Assume that the extensions on the Investment Summary on the handwritten draft are correct. However, there may be other errors in this source document. Use proofreaders' marks to mark needed changes in the printed copy. Refer to the calendar on page 130.

April 10, 19--

Dr. Alfred Harrison, Jr., PA
4156 O'Harra Avenue
Charleston, SC 29405

Dear Dr. Harrison:

This letter confirms our resent discussion concerning the changes that we made in the stock portfolio for your medical practice. The attached information shows the various quantitys and prices of each security sold on March 14, 13, and 15. The total amount received for these transactions were $132,330.97.

The information also shows that the market value for these securities at the close of business on January 13 was $143,465.25. This increase of $11,139.28 has come over a ten-month period.

Even with the recent gain in the market this investment change has been correct for you. The interest, appreciation, and tax advantages gained by changing your investment strategy will increase your income significantly.

I look forward to our meeting two weeks from today, Monday, April 25, at 10:00 a.m. in our conference room. Please plan to have lunch with me.

Sincerely yours,

Charles D. Lindquist

bdr

Enclosure

cc: Jeff Renslow, Ms. Helen Valient, and Ralph Townshend

BRENNER, BRENNER, AND PEREZ
Investment Summary
Dr. Alfred Harrison, Jr., PA

Date Sold	Number	Symbol	Price	Total Amount	Price 1/13/--	Market Value
3/13/--	400	BAC	19 1/4	$ 7,521.68	14 5/8	$ 5,850.00
3/13/--	400	XON	49	19,268.96	54 1/4	21,700.00
3/14/--	100	LOF	48	4,699.33	48 1/2	4,850.00
3/14/--	100	NSP	42 3/4	4,181.53	50 1/8	5,012.50
3/14/--	200	NSP	42 3/4	8,381.27	50 1/8	10,025.00
3/14/--	20	NSP	42 5/8	838.16	50 1/8	1,002.50
3/14/--	300	RJR	84 7/8	25,161.65	31 5/8	23,756.25
3/14/--	400	SN	63 1/4	24,910.65	60 3/8	24,150.00
3/14/--	700	STY	29 1/8	20,022.44	37	25,900.00
3/14/--	87	STY	29 1/8	2,499.56	37	3,219.00
3/14/--	300	WPC	31 5/8	9,295.74	38 1/2	11,550.00
3/15/--	200	SFX	27 3/4	5,550.00	32 1/2	6,500.00
3/15/--	108	SFX	26 3/4	2,889.00	32 1/2	3,510.00
			Totals	$ 132,330.97		$ 143,465.25

BRENNER, BRENNER & PEREZ

| Post Office Box 2253 | Charleston, South Carolina 29405 | (803) 555-3062 |

April 10, 19--

Dr. Alfred Harrison, Jr., PA
4156 O'Harra Avenue
Charleston, SC 29405

Dear Mr. Harrison:

   This letter confirms our resent discussion concerning the changes
that we made in the stock portfolio for your medical practice. The
attached information shows the various quantitys and prices of each security sold on March 14, 13, and 15. The total amount received for these
transactions were $132,330.97.

   The information also shows that the market value for these
securities at the close of business on January 13 was $143,465.25. This
increase of $11,139.28 has come over a ten-month period.

   Even with the recent gain in the market this investment change has
has been correct for you. The interest, appreciation, and tax advantages
gained by changing your investment strategy will increase your income
significantly.

I look forward to our meeting two weeks from today, Monday, April 25,
at 10:00 a.m. inour conference room. Please plan to have lunch with me.

                              Sincerely Yours,

                              Charles D. Lindquist

bdr

Enclosure
cc: Jeff Renslow, Ms. Helen Valient, and Ralph Townshend

BRENNER, BRENNER, AND PEREZ

Investment Summary

Dr. Alfred Harrison, Jr., PA

Date Sold	Number	Symbol	Price	Total Amount	Price 1/13/--	Market Value
3/13/--	400	BAC	19 1/4	$ 7,521.68	14 5/8	$ 5,850.00
3/13/--	400	XON	49	19,268.96	54 1/4	21,700.00
3-14/--	100	LOF	48	4,699.33	48 1/2	4,850.00
3/14/--	100	NSP	42 3/4	4,181.35	50 1/8	5,012.50
3/14/--	200	NSP	42 3/4	8,381.27	50 1/8	10,025.00
3/14/--	20	NSP	42 5/8	838.16	50 1/8	1,002.50
3/14/--	300	RJR	84 7/8	25,161.65	31 5/8	23,756.25
3/14/--	400	SN	63 1/4	24,910.65	60 3/8	24,150.00
3/14/--	70	STY	29 1/8	20,022.44	37	25,900.00
3/14/--	87	STY	29 1/8	2,499.56	37	3,219.00
3/14/--	300	WCP	31 5/8	9,295.74	38 1/2	11,550.00
3/15/--	200	SFX	27 3/4	5,550.00	32 1/2	6,500.00
3/15/--	108	SFX	26 3/4	2,889.00	32 1/2	3,510.00
			Totals	$132,330.97		$143,465.25

Student Software Manual

Sue C. Camp
Joseph Tinervia

This manual is to be used in conjunction with DEVELOPING PROOFREADING SKILL SOFTWARE, which is available for the IBM PC, Apple IIe and IIc, TRS-80 Models III and 4, IBM Displaywriter, and Wang OIS.

Contents

Introduction

By doing the exercises in the DEVELOPING PROOFREADING SKILL text-workbook, you have gotten a lot of practice in proofreading paper documents using a pen and pencil. You have been trained to spot errors in printed, handwritten, and typed documents.

On the job, however, proofreading is not limited to checking one paper document against another. Office workers who use word processing systems are expected to proofread copy on screen and to correct errors before documents are printed. Word processing has made document production more efficient, but to take advantage of this efficiency proofread and correct on screen before printing.

DEVELOPING PROOFREADING SKILL SOFTWARE will provide you with an opportunity to practice your proofreading and word processing skills. Using a word processing system with which you are already familiar, you will retrieve, proofread, correct, and print the business documents contained in the software.

The first part of the diskette contains 13 files—an introduction and 12 documents to be proofread that correspond to the 12 chapters in the text-workbook. The second part is a practice set. It consists of a variety of documents prepared by the Classified Advertising Department of *The Daily Ledger*, a Chicago-area newspaper.

All the documents in the software have been given file names. For a list of the file names used with your word processing system, refer to the appropriate document record sheet on pages 146–149. For example, if you are using MultiMate on an IBM PC, locate the document record sheet for the IBM PC on page 147. That record sheet will tell you the file names used with MultiMate on the IBM PC. Keep the document record sheet handy when you are proofreading;

you will need these file names in order to retrieve the documents you will proofread.

▼▼ Proofreading Pointers

▼ Make sure you are retrieving the correct document. Keep your document record sheet handy.

▼ Correct errors on screen carefully, and save your revised document to your own diskette before you print a copy.

▼ Print copies of letters, memos, and so on after you have proofread, corrected, formatted (if applicable), and saved the documents properly.

▼ Proofread each document again after it is printed. If you find additional errors, correct the errors on your diskette, save the document again, and print a revised copy to submit to your instructor.

Directions for Part 1— Chapter Applications

Note: See the document record sheets on pages 146–149 for a list of document file names for your word processing system.

CHAPTER 1: TYPOGRAPHICAL ERRORS

On page 150 is a list of sales representatives arranged by region. *All the information on this list is correct.* Load the Chapter 1 application and proofread the list of sales representatives, which has been rearranged in order of sales volume, against the information in the list on page 150. Correct any errors on the screen, print a copy of the corrected list, and submit the list to your instructor.

CHAPTER 2: MORE TYPOGRAPHICAL ERRORS

Correct the transposition, spacing, omission, and repetition errors in this letter. Print one copy of the corrected letter and submit it to your instructor.

CHAPTER 3: PROOFREADERS' MARKS

Proofread the keyboarded employee bulletin against the rough-draft copy on pages 151–152. *The rough draft is correct.*
　　Proceed as follows:
1. Print a copy of the uncorrected Chapter 3 file and mark all your corrections on the printout using standard proofreaders' marks.
2. Following the marked-up printout, correct the document on your diskette.
3. Print one copy of the corrected file.
4. Submit both your marked-up copy and your final printout to your instructor.

CHAPTER 4: NUMBER ALERTNESS

As you proofread the memo to store managers, check carefully for errors in number usage. Print a corrected copy of the memo.

CHAPTER 5: STYLES AND FORMATS FOR LETTERS AND MEMOS

Correct any format errors in the letter in the Chapter 5 file, and print one copy of the letter in block style.

Then reformat the letter in modified-block style with indented paragraphs, print one copy, and submit it to your instructor along with the block-style letter.

CHAPTER 6: CAPITALIZATION ALERTNESS

Correct any capitalization errors in the memo to Jim Muncy. Check the style of the memo to make sure that it conforms to standard memo style. Print a corrected copy of the memo.

CHAPTER 7: COMMA USAGE

Correct any errors in comma usage in the letter to Andrea Sarto. Then print a corrected copy of the letter.

CHAPTER 8: SPELLING AND WORD DIVISION

Correct any errors in spelling, word division, plurals, and possessives in this draft copy of a memo to the district managers. Then print a final copy, correctly formatted.

CHAPTER 9: GRAMMAR ALERTNESS

Proofread the letter to Robert Duke for sentence fragments, subject-verb agreement, and parallel construction. Correct each error; then print one corrected copy of the letter.

CHAPTER 10: PUNCTUATION ALERTNESS

The marketing manager for your firm has asked you to proofread the rough draft of an ad that will be placed in a popular computer magazine. Correct any punctuation errors as you read the ad copy, and print a double-spaced corrected draft.

CHAPTER 11: PROOFREADING STATISTICAL AND TECHNICAL DOCUMENTS

On pages 153–154 you will find correct copy for several sections of the Fidelity Company's catalog. Proofread the keyboarded copy on the diskette against the copy on pages 153–154. Make any necessary corrections, and print the corrected copy for your instructor.

CHAPTER 12: CORRECTING INCONSISTENCIES

Proofread the letter to Helen Montross, paying special attention to inconsistencies. If two items are inconsistent, assume the first one is correct and fix the second one. Print a corrected copy of the letter.

Directions for Part 2—
THE DAILY LEDGER,
A Proofreading Practice Set

You are employed in the Classified Advertising Department of THE DAILY LEDGER, a large Chicago-area newspaper. As part of your duties, you proofread classified ads to make sure that each ad accurately reflects the advertiser's original copy. In addition, your manager, Marsha Chin, often gives you other responsibilities. For example, she has asked you to assist her in a special mailing she is now planning. (THE DAILY LEDGER was recently named the number one

144

newspaper for classified advertising in the Chicago area, and Marsha plans to take advantage of this fact by sending a special promotional letter to the LEDGER'S top ten clients.)

HOW TO PROCEED

On your diskette are six project files. Consult the document record sheet for your word processing system for the file names. Below is an explanation of what each file contains and what you are to do with each file.

PROJECT 1

On page 155 is a list of the "Top 10 Classified Ad Clients." All the information on that list is correct. Proofread the alphabetized, keyboarded list in the software to make sure that all the client names, addresses, telephone numbers, and account numbers match precisely. Double-check that the list is in proper alphabetical order by company name.

Correct any errors you find on the screen display, print one copy of the corrected listing, and submit it to your instructor.

PROJECT 2

Copy for six ads that was delivered by messenger for inclusion in the next edition of the LEDGER appears on pages 156–157. All the ad information there is correct.

At the end of each ad is a client account number, which identifies which ad belongs to which client. In the Project 2 file, however, the account number should be replaced with the client's company name and phone number. The company name should be in all-capital letters on the last line of each ad, followed by four spaces and the phone number (omit the area code); for example:

SKLAR CHRYSLER-PLYMOUTH   555-1200

Use the "Top 10 Classified Ad Clients" from Project 1 to check the correct names and numbers.

PROJECT 3

A rough-draft copy of a letter that will be sent to the top ten clients listed in Project 1 is shown on page 158. Proofread the keyboarded copy in the Project 3 file against the rough draft, correcting any errors on the screen.

Add the following to the letter:

1. Today's date.
2. Your manager's name and title below "Sincerely":
   Marsha P. Chin
   Manager, Classified Advertising
3. Your reference initials and an enclosure notation.

Then add the inside address and salutation for each of the ten clients, print one letter for each client, and submit all ten letters to your instructor.

PROJECT 4

Marsha has given you ad copy (see the Project 4 file) and has asked you to correct any errors and make any style changes required. In addition, the line rate for each type of ad must be increased by 10 cents.

Print the corrected ad copy, and submit it to your instructor.

PROJECT 5

As Marsha left the office on a business trip, she asked you to read and correct a memo she wrote to John R. Walters, executive vice president of advertising for THE DAILY LEDGER. Retrieve the Project 5 file for the draft of her memo.

Correct any errors in the memo. (Wherever two facts are inconsistent, assume that the first is correct.) Then print a copy in correct memo format, and submit the final copy to your instructor.

PROJECT 6

To speed up the process of placing ads, THE DAILY LEDGER has a staff of ad specialists who keyboard ad copy directly from clients on the telephone. The four ads in the Project 6 file were taken by telephone.

During certain times, the ad specialists get many calls and must work under pressure. To make sure that they record all ad copy completely, they often use abbreviations for words that are commonly used in ads, such as the following:

dept	department
sal	salary
exp	experience
applic	applicant
cand	candidate
exc	excellent
prev	previous
comm	commission
comp	company

In addition, they use the symbol / to indicate a new paragraph.

Proofread the four ads carefully. Make sure that you spell out all abbreviations and correct any errors that the ad specialists made in keyboarding the copy hastily. Print one copy of the corrected ads, and submit the printout to your instructor.

Apple IIe/IIc Document Record Sheet

Application		AppleWorks File Name	Apple Writer II File Name*	PFS:Write File Name
Introduction		INTRO1 INTRO2	INTRO	INTRO1
Chapter 1	Typographical Errors	C1	C1	C1
Chapter 2	More Typographical Errors	C2	C2	C2
Chapter 3	Proofreaders' Marks	C3	C3	C3
Chapter 4	Number Alertness	C4	C4	C4
Chapter 5	Letters and Memos	C5	C5	C5
Chapter 6	Capitalization Alertness	C6	C6	C6
Chapter 7	Comma Usage	C7	C7	C7
Chapter 8	Spelling and Word Division	C8	C8	C8
Chapter 9	Grammar Alertness	C9	C9	C9
Chapter 10	Punctuation Alertness	C10	C10	C10
Chapter 11	Statistical and Technical Documents	C11	C11	C11
Chapter 12	Correcting Inconsistencies	C12	C12	C12

Practice Set

Application	AppleWorks File Name	Apple Writer II File Name*	PFS:Write File Name
Project 1	PR1	PR1	PR1
Project 2	PR2	PR2	PR2
Project 3	PR3	PR3	PR3
Project 4	PR4	PR4	PR4
Project 5	PR5	PR5	PR5
Project 6	PR6	PR6	PR6

*Apple Writer II users must prefix the file name with the volume name (CAMP on the original diskette). In addition, three files should be retrieved for each application: for example, /CAMP/C1, /CAMP/TABS/C1, and /CAMP/PRT/C1 (the text, tabs, and print files for application C1).

IBM PC Document Record Sheet

Application		DisplayWrite 3 File Name	MultiMate File Name	PFS:Write File Name	WordStar File Name
Introduction		**DWINTRO**	**MMINTRO**	**PFSINTRO**	**WSINTRO**
Chapter 1	Typographical Errors	DWC1	MMC1	PFSC1	WSC1
Chapter 2	More Typographical Errors	DWC2	MMC2	PFSC2	WSC2
Chapter 3	Proofreaders' Marks	DWC3	MMC3	PFSC3	WSC3
Chapter 4	Number Alertness	DWC4	MMC4	PFSC4	WSC4
Chapter 5	Letters and Memos	DWC5	MMC5	PFSC5	WSC5
Chapter 6	Capitalization Alertness	DWC6	MMC6	PFSC6	WSC6
Chapter 7	Comma Usage	DWC7	MMC7	PFSC7	WSC7
Chapter 8	Spelling and Word Division	DWC8	MMC8	PFSC8	WSC8
Chapter 9	Grammar Alertness	DWC9	MMC9	PFSC9	WSC9
Chapter 10	Punctuation Alertness	DWC10	MMC10	PFSC10	WSC10
Chapter 11	Statistical and Technical Documents	DWC11	MMC11	PFSC11	WSC11
Chapter 12	Correcting Inconsistencies	DWC12	MMC12	PFSC12	WSC12

Practice Set

Application	DisplayWrite 3 File Name	MultiMate File Name	PFS:Write File Name	WordStar File Name
Project 1	DWPR1	MMPR1	PFSPR1	WSPR1
Project 2	DWPR2	MMPR2	PFSPR2	WSPR2
Project 3	DWPR3	MMPR3	PFSPR3	WSPR3
Project 4	DWPR4	MMPR4	PFSPR4	WSPR4
Project 5	DWPR5	MMPR5	PFSPR5	WSPR5
Project 6	DWPR6	MMPR6	PFSPR6	WSPR6

148

IBM Displaywriter Document Record

Application		File Name
Introduction		INTRO
Chapter 1	Typographical Errors	C1
Chapter 2	More Typographical Errors	C2
Chapter 3	Proofreaders' Marks	C3
Chapter 4	Number Alertness	C4
Chapter 5	Letters and Memos	C5
Chapter 6	Capitalization Alertness	C6
Chapter 7	Comma Usage	C7
Chapter 8	Spelling and Word Division	C8
Chapter 9	Grammar Alertness	C9
Chapter 10	Punctuation Alertness	C10
Chapter 11	Statistical and Technical Documents	C11
Chapter 12	Correcting Inconsistencies	C12
Practice Set		
Project 1		PR1
Project 2		PR2
Project 3		PR3
Project 4		PR4
Project 5		PR5
Project 6		PR6

TRS-80 Model III and 4 Document Record Sheet

Application		File Name
Introduction		INTRO
Chapter 1	Typographical Errors	C1
Chapter 2	More Typographical Errors	C2
Chapter 3	Proofreaders' Marks	C3
Chapter 4	Number Alertness	C4
Chapter 5	Letters and Memos	C5
Chapter 6	Capitalization Alertness	C6
Chapter 7	Comma Usage	C7
Chapter 8	Spelling and Word Division	C8
Chapter 9	Grammar Alertness	C9
Chapter 10	Punctuation Alertness	C10
Chapter 11	Statistical and Technical Documents	C11
Chapter 12	Correcting Inconsistencies	C12
Practice Set		
Project 1		PR1
Project 2		PR2
Project 3		PR3
Project 4		PR4
Project 5		PR5
Project 6		PR6

Wang OIS Document Record Sheet

Application		Name	Number on Original Diskette	Number After Super-copying
Introduction		INTRO		
Chapter 1	Typographical Errors	C1	_____	_____
Chapter 2	More Typographical Errors	C2	_____	_____
Chapter 3	Proofreaders' Marks	C3	_____	_____
Chapter 4	Number Alertness	C4	_____	_____
Chapter 5	Letters and Memos	C5	_____	_____
Chapter 6	Capitalization Alertness	C6	_____	_____
Chapter 7	Comma Usage	C7	_____	_____
Chapter 8	Spelling and Word Division	C8	_____	_____
Chapter 9	Grammar Alertness	C9	_____	_____
Chapter 10	Punctuation Alertness	C10	_____	_____
Chapter 11	Statistical and Technical Documents	C11	_____	_____
Chapter 12	Correcting Inconsistencies	C12	_____	_____
Practice Set				
Project 1		PR1	_____	_____
Project 2		PR2	_____	_____
Project 3		PR3	_____	_____
Project 4		PR4	_____	_____
Project 5		PR5	_____	_____
Project 6		PR6	_____	_____

TOP SALES REPRESENTATIVES BY REGION

Sales Representative	Volume for Period Jan. 1–June 30
Region 1	
Buckley, Amanda (Rep. No. 183) 12 Watson Drive Lodi, NJ 07644	$1,412,500
Coronella, Mario J. (Rep. No. 127) One Canterbury Avenue Pittsburgh, PA 15219	$1,450,750
Elmendorf, Jack W. (Rep. No. 137) 75 Channing Street Frostburg, MD 21532	$1,501,100
Monson, Diane R. (Rep. No. 144) 1100 Highland Boulevard Greenville, NC 27834	$1,485,000
Plante, Hiram (Rep. No. 121) 32 Dudley Court Decatur, MS 39327	$1,458,700
Shallcross, Bette Jean (Rep. No. 149) 41 Madison Avenue Athens, OH 45701	$1,375,000
Region 2	
Gunn, Millard J. (Rep. No. 231) 700 West Broad Street Kalamazoo, MI 49074	$1,415,000
Pellegrino, Andrew (Rep. No. 232) 198 Sherwood Parkway Rochester, MN 55901	$1,475,650
Urbanowski, Claire (Rep. No. 276) 86 Ridge Way Salina, KS 67401	$1,350,875
Region 3	
Aaron, Orville W. (Rep. No. 370) 719 Lawrence Avenue San Luis Obispo, CA 93401	$1,470,000
Desmond, Harriet T. (Rep. No. 314) 12 South Avenue Yuma, AZ 85634	$1,370,850
Spellman, Jessica (Rep. No. 341) 611 Woodland Avenue Spokane Falls, WA 99204	$1,501,400

TRAVEL TIPS

(Bulletin No. 123: "Fire Safety in Hotels")

Following safety precautions when in hotels can help save your life. Last year, our employees stayed overnight in hotels more than 500,000 times. For the protection of our staff members while they're away on business trips, the Security Department has compiled some tips concerning hotel fires.

The by-products of fires--gases, smoke, and panic--are responsible for killing more people than the flames themselves. Prepare yourself for your overnight trips by planning an escape route as soon as you check in your hotel. After you've checked in, be sure that you can answer these five questions:

Where are the fire exits on your floor?

What are their locations?

Which exit is CLOSEST to your room?

Where are the fire extinguishers on your floor?

Do you know how to operate that kind of extinguisher?

Your ability to answer such questions may save your life. In addition, be sure to follow these helpful tips:

1. Do _not_ smoke in bed. A burning cigarette is not only dangerous but often fatal. As a result of jet

lag, travelers may be more tired than usual and may be more likely to fall asleep while smoking.

2. If you smell smoke, call the hotel operator and investigate the cause of the smell.

3. If there IS a fire (or if you strongly suspect that there is), feel the door or the doorknob for heat BEFORE you open the door. A hot door or doorknob might indicate a fire outside the door——a sign that you should NOT open the door.

4. In case of fire, do NOT use the elevators. Instead, you should use the fire stairs to exit.

5. Be sure to take your room key if you do leave the room. Reason: In a fire, you may be forced to return to your room.

6. CRAWL to the fire exit nearest your room. Reason: The air nearer the floor may be safer for you to breathe.

A more-detailed booklet of informational tips has been developed by our Security Department. For a copy of this booklet, call Extension 4300.

F I D E L I T Y
C A L C U L A T O R S

FC420/56 "The Scientific Brain"

* 66 scientific functions and 10 physical constants
* RAM: 4K bytes (expandable to 8K bytes with two FX900/67 RAM cards)
* ROM: 28K bytes
* Display: 24 alphanumeric characters
* DC power: two lithium batteries (FB300/456)
* Programming language: BASIC
* Dimensions: 5/8" H x 7 3/8" W x 3 1/4" D
* Weight: 8.9 oz
* Price: $99.99

FC418/27 Commercial Desktop Printing Calculator

* 12-digit printer/display
* Decimal point system: 0, 1, 2, 3, F (full float), and ADD(2) mode positions; 5/4 round-off or round-down
* Dimensions: 10.2" W x 12.6" D x 4" H
* Weight: 5.1 lbs
* Price: $124.95

FC430/49 Compact Printer

* 10 digits
* Full decimal system: floating, fixed (0-3) with round-off, and ADD mode
* AC (FZ900/67 adaptor, optional) or DC (four AA batteries)
* Printer paper: standard 2 1/4" paper
* Easy-to-replace ink-roll cartridge (FIR120/50)
* Dimensions: 2" H x 9" W x 4 3/4" D
* Weight: 1.2 lbs
* Price: $34.95

F I D E L I T Y
CALCULATOR ACCESSORIES

FZ900/67 Printer AC adaptor
. . . .$19.95

FC910/45 2 1/4" Printer paper
(box of 12) $9.95

FIR120/50 Ink-roll cartridge
(box of 12) $7.95

FB300/456 Lithium battery
. . . .$6.95

F I D E L I T Y
LETTER-QUALITY PRINTERS

FQ109/790 and FQ109/791 Printers

* Interface: Parallel-Centronics compatible
* Printing direction: Bidirectional
* Pitch: 10, 12, 15, and PS Paper width: 17"
* Printing speed: Model FQ109/790, 20 CPS; Model FQ109/791, 36 CPS
* Power rating: 90-120 V, AC 50-60 Hz
* Dimensions: 22.9" H x 7.8" W x 14.9" D
* Weight: Model FQ109/790, 31.9 lbs; Model FQ109/791, 32.8 lbs
* Prices: Model FQ109/790, $459.95; Model FQ109/791, $839.95

F I D E L I T Y
PRINTER ACCESSORIES

FT109/101 Tractor feed
. . . .$124.95

FT109/110 Cut-sheet feeder
. . . .$199.95

FM200/620 Multistrike ribbons
(box of 6). $49.95

F I D E L I T Y
ELECTRONIC TYPEWRITERS

FET319/510 "The Typemaster"

* 96-character keyboard
* 15-character liquid crystal
  display
* 500-character memory
* Automatic centering
* Pitch: 10, 12, 15, and PS
* Typing speed: 15 CPS
* Can be connected (via FIF325/90)
  to computer system for 20 CPS,
  bidirectional printout
* Dimensions: 17 1/4" W x 15 1/2" D
  x 5 1/2" H
* Weight: 19.8 lbs
* Price: $629.50

F I D E L I T Y
TYPEWRITER ACCESSORIES

FR300/721 Black correctable
carbon
(box of 12). $49.95

FR300/722 Green correctable
carbon
(box of 12). $49.95

FR300/723 Blue correctable
carbon
(box of 12). $49.95

FR300/724 Brown correctable
carbon
(box of 12). $49.95

FR300/725 Red correctable carbon
(box of 12). $49.95

FR300/729 Black multistrike
ribbon
(box of 12). $69.95

FIF325/90 Computer interface
. . . . $129.95

TOP 10 CLASSIFIED AD CLIENTS

Ms. Barbara V. Goodell-Perkins
WALLACE LINCOLN-FORD
221 South LaSalle Street
Chicago, IL 60607
  Tel. (312) 555-4500
  Acct. No. 198-676-4

Mr. J. W. Herrmann
LION REAL ESTATE, INC.
1578 North Michigan Avenue
Chicago, IL 60616
  Tel. (312) 555-0400
  Acct. No. 211-044-0

Mrs. Roberta T. Slawinski
COLE/SAMPSON/TRENT TEMPORARIES
1919 North Crawford
  Chicago, Il 60621
  Tel. (312) 555-7500
  Acct. No. 198-750-5

Dr. Lizabeth Waugh
THE WAUGH SCHOOL FOR BUSINESS
125 East Lake Avenue
Chicago, IL 60610
  Tel. (312) 555-4565
  Acct. No. 121-443-4

Mr. Andrew T. Sloane
THE SLOANE-RICHARDS AGENCY
100 East Ohio
Chicago, IL 60606
  Tel. (312) 555-8900
  Acct. No. 198-677-9

Mr. Walter J. Smigelski
NORRIS IMPORTED AUTOMOBILES
141 East Walton
Chicago, Il 60619
  Tel. (312) 555-9072
  Acct. No. 198-987-7

Ms. Jeanette Sklar
SKLAR CHRYSLER-PLYMOUTH
1400 East 9th Street
Chicago, IL 60617
  Tel. (312) 555-1200
  Acct. No. 211-600-3

Mr. Jerome P. Koenig
ADVANCE PERSONNEL AGENCY
1600 Spartan Drive
Elgin, Il 60120
  Tel. (312) 555-3575
  Acct. No. 189-577-6

Mr. William Van Arsdale Jr.
DENNIS & AMATO PERSONNEL INC.
120 South Michigan Avenue
Chicago, IL 60617
  Tel. (312) 555-7842
  Acct. No. 210-012-2

Ms. Maria T. Risoli
THE ACADEMY OF BUSINESS
75 East Williamsport
Rockford, IL 61101
Tel. (312) 555-4930
Acct. No. 202-371-0

Ad 1

PEACE, PRIVACY, AND TRANQUILITY!

See for yourself how peaceful, private, and tranquil this
beautiful four-bedroom ranch home can be. Immaculately
kept, this home is in move-in condition. It's surrounded by
tall oaks, and it's very elegantly landscaped. All
this--and central air too--for only $89,900.
Acct. No. 211-044-0

Ad 2

1985 Lincoln Town Car

Pearl gray, four-door Town Car has automatic transmission,
power steering/windows/brakes/seats, cruise control, AM/FM
cassette radio, leather seats, and much, ~~much~~ more. Only   (STET)
15,000 miles. Asking $19,000.
Acct. No. 198-676-4

Ad 3

ASSISTANT PRODUCT MANAGER

If you'd like to take advantage of a superb entry-level
marketing position in a Fortune 500 company, this may be the
spot for you. The Marketing Department manager of one of
the nation's foremost food companies requires a
well-organized, hard-working individual with good
interpersonal skills and at least one year of marketing
experience. If you qualify, call for an appointment. Ask
for Mr. Van Arsdale.
Acct. No. 210-012-2

Ad 4

<u>Elegant English Tudor</u>

This 20-year=old home offers a *formal* dining room, ~~a~~ spacious living
room with a wood=burning fireplace, ~~a~~ double=oven kitchen, family
room, enclosed porch, and four huge bedrooms. As if this weren't
enough, its boast natural woodwork and a two=car garage. Asking
$149,000.
Acct. No. 211-044-0

Ad 5

<u>Ridgewood Corporate Park</u> II

It's prime location ensures *that* Ridgewood Corporate Park II *will* match the
~~success~~ *popularity* of it's predecessor. It offers easy ~~excess~~ access to all major
highways and exceptionally spacious parking facility. Suits with
corner locations and tremendous window exposure, *are* ~~is~~ available at
below=market rates. ¶ Call Andrew Sloan to arrange an appointment to
inspect this ~~this~~ site and see for yourself, why Ridgewood Corporate
park II is the place for your head quarters.
Acct. No. 198-677-9

Ad 6

DREAMING ABOUT *YOUR* ~~THE~~ FUTURE?

If you're thinking about your future, now's the time to consider
some of the rewarding opportunitys that exists in today's Business
World. The <u>Academy of Business</u> has been training men and women   *and has a*
for more than 30 years, ¶ Course offerings include word   *superb faculty—*
processing, medical secretarial, legal secretarial, travel and   *all of whom are*
tourism, and electronics and *computer* technology. / For more information ¶ *businessmen and*
call The <u>Academy of Business</u>—or better yet, visit us today!   *businesswomen.*
Acct. No. 202-371-0

Dear   :

Perhaps you have already ~~have~~ heard that The Daily
Ledger was named by the Central Newspaper Association,
as this area's leading newspaper for classified
advertising. According to the CNA report (a copy is
enclosed for you to read,) more people place--and
read--classifieds in The Dialy Ledger than any other local
paper. As a result, your Daily Ledger classified ad
reaches 20% more reader's than it would reach in any other
local paper. Because the cost of advertising in the
Ledger is the same as in other papers, you are
effectively, saving 20% on your advertising expenses when
you place you're ads in The Daily Ledger.

Please read the enclosed copy of the CNA report so that
you can hear ~~from~~ an independent source say, ~~tell you why~~
"it pays to advertise in The Daily Ledger."

Sincerely,

Index

159